5|11|10
$16.00
B&T
AS
14dg

THE BOOK OF WHAT REMAINS

ALSO BY BENJAMIN ALIRE SÁENZ

POETRY

Dreaming the End of War

Elegies in Blue

Dark and Perfect Angels

Calendar of Dust

FICTION

Last Night I Sang to the Monster

He Forgot to Say Goodbye

In Perfect Light

Sammy and Juliana in Hollywood

The House of Forgetting

Carry Me Like Water

Flowers for the Broken

CHILDREN'S BOOKS

The Dog Who Loved Tortillas

A Perfect Season for Dreaming

Grandma Fina and Her Wonderful Umbrellas

A Gift from Papá Diego

THE BOOK OF WHAT REMAINS
BENJAMIN ALIRE SÁENZ

COPPER CANYON PRESS

PORT TOWNSEND, WASHINGTON

Cover art: Photograph by Benjamin Alire Sáenz

Copper Canyon Press is in residence at Fort Worden State Park in Port Townsend, Washington, under the auspices of Centrum. Centrum is a gathering place for artists and creative thinkers from around the world, students of all ages and backgrounds, and audiences seeking extraordinary cultural enrichment.

LIBRARY OF CONGRESS CATALOGING-IN-PUBLICATION DATA
Sáenz, Benjamin Alire.
 The book of what remains / Benjamin Alire Sáenz.
   p. cm.
ISBN 978-1-55659-297-3 (pbk. : alk. paper)
 I. Title.

PS3569.A27B66 2010
811'.54—dc22

                                        2009041600

98765432 first printing

COPPER CANYON PRESS
Post Office Box 271
Port Townsend, Washington 98368
www.coppercanyonpress.org

The poems are set in Janson, originally designed by Miklós (Nicholas) Kis circa 1685. The headings are set in DinEngschrift, a variation of DIN 1451, designed by Akira Kobayashi of Linotype. DIN is an acronym for the Deutsches Institut für Normung (German Institute for Standardization) and the name of a sans serif typeface family. In 1936 the German Standard Committee selected DIN 1451 as the standard typeface for use in the areas of engineering, technology, traffic, administration, and business.

for Hector and Annie

whom I have loved all my life

CONTENTS

The Book of What Remains

Prologue

A writer is being interviewed on the radio. He has written a book, *Proust Was a Neuroscientist*. I do not like Proust and so I am not really listening— but then something happens *and I am listening*. The man begins talking about the nature of memories and how they change. They change because we change them. He says this is a fact. I have no reason to believe him. Neither do I have any reason to doubt him. He has written this book so he must be some kind of expert. According to this expert, every time we visit a memory, we change it. If we are to believe the findings of this erudite, disciplined, and articulate scholar, then we must conclude that over the course of our lives, we completely change every memory we visit. The final result is that there is no purity to remembering. Memories, he says, are beautifully sincere. They also lie. The interviewer's response interests me. "That's so sad," she says. I do not share her sense of sadness. The fact that our memories may be half-truths doesn't break my heart. There is a litany of sadder things—much, much sadder things—that have broken my heart. There is no need to be specific. Is there?

But now that I am on the subject of memories, I am thinking that even *if* memories lie, even *if* no memory is true, despite all of that, there must be some truth that remains—even within the lie. And that truth is what I'm hanging on to. That is all that remains.

The Book of War and Living

For me, the war began when I was born.

PANCHO VILLA

Meditation on Living in the Desert

NO. I

The rains do not always come.
The winds remain.

The dust will gather on your tongue.

Confessions: My Father, Hummingbirds, and Frantz Fanon

Every effort is made to bring the colonised
person to admit the inferiority of his culture.

FRANTZ FANON

                    And there are days when storms hover
Over my house, their brooding just this side of rage,
An open hand about to slap a face. You won't believe me

When I tell you it is *not* personal. *It isn't.* It only feels
That way *because the face is yours.* So what if it is the only
Face you've got? Listen, a storm will grab the first thing
In its path, a Persian cat, a sixth-grade boy on his way home
From school, an old woman watering her roses, a black
Man running down a street (late to a dinner with his wife),
A white guy buying cigarettes at the corner store. A storm
Will grab a young woman trying to escape her boyfriend,
A garbage can, a Mexican busboy with no papers, *you.*
We are all collateral damage for someone's beautiful
Ideology, all of us inanimate in the face of the onslaught.
My father had the biggest hands I've ever seen. He never
Wore a wedding ring. Somehow, it would have looked lost,
Misplaced on his thick worker's hands that were, to me,
As large as Africa. There have been a good many storms
In Africa over the centuries. One was called *colonialism*
(Though I confess to loving Tarzan as a boy).

                              In my thirties,
I read a book by Frantz Fanon. I fell in love
With the storms in his book even though they broke
My heart and made me want to scream. What good
Is screaming? Even a bad actress in a horror flick
Can do that. In my twenties, I had fallen in love

With the storms in the essays of James Baldwin.
They were like perfect poems. His friends called
Him Jimmy. People didn't think he was beautiful.
Oh God, but he was. He could make a hand that was
Slapping you into something that was loving, loving you.
He could make rage sound elegant. Have you ever
Read "Stranger in the Village"? How would you like
To feel like a fucking storm every time someone looked
At *you?*

                                                One time I was
At a party. Some guy asked me: *What are you, anyway?*
I downed my beer. *Mexican* I said. *Really* he said. *Do*
You play soccer? No I said *but I drink tequila.* He smiled
At me, *That's cool.* I smiled back *So what are you?*
What do you think I am he said. *An asshole* I said. People
Hate you when you're right. Especially if you're Mexican.
And every time I leave town, I pray that people will stop
Repeating *You're from El Paso* with that same tone
Of voice they use when they see a rat running across
Their living room, interrupting their second glass
Of scotch. My father's dead (though sometimes I wake
And swear he has never been more alive—especially when
I see him staring back at me as I shave in the morning).
Even though I understand something about hating a man
I have never really understood the logic of slavery.
What do I know? I don't particularly like the idea of cheap
Labor. I don't like guns. And I don't even believe
White men are superior. Do you? I wanted to be
Saint Francis. I took this ambition very seriously. Instead
I wound up becoming a middle-aged man who dreams
Storms where all the animals wind up dead. It scares
Me to think I have this dream inside me. Still,
I love dogs—even mean ones. I could forgive
A dog that bit me. But if a man bit me, that would be
Another story. I have made my peace with cats.

I am especially in love with hummingbirds (though
They're as mean as roosters in a cockfight). Have
You ever seen the storms in the eyes of men who
Were betting on a cockfight?

                         Last night, there was hail, thunder,
A tornado touching down in the desert—though I was
Away and was not a firsthand witness. I was in another
Place, listening to the waves of the ocean crash against
The shore. Sometimes I think the sea is angry. Who
Can blame it? There are a million things to be angry
About. Have you noticed that some people don't give
A damn and just keep on shopping? Doesn't that make you
Angry? A storm is like God. You don't have to see it
To believe—sometimes you just have to place
Your faith in it. When my father walked into a room
It felt like that. Like the crashing waves. You know,
Like a storm. This is the truth of the matter: I am
The son of a storm. Look, everyone has to be the son
Of something. The thing to do when you are caught
In the middle of a storm is to abandon your car,
Keep quiet. Pray. Wait. Tell that to the men
Who were sleeping on the *Arizona* when
The Japanese dropped their bombs. War is the worst
Kind of storm. The truth is I have never met a breathing
Human being who did not have at least one scar
On his body. Bombs and bullets do more than leave
A permanent mark on the skin. I have never liked
The expression *They were out for blood.*

                             There are days
When there are so many storms hovering around
My house that I cannot even see the blue in the sky.
My father loved the sky. He was trying to memorize
The clouds before he died. I confess to being
Jealous of the sky.

                    On Sunday mornings
I picture Frantz Fanon as an old man. He is looking up
At the pure African sky. He is trying to imagine how it appeared
Before the white men came. I don't want to dream all the dead
Animals we have made extinct. I want to dream a sky
Full of hummingbirds. I would like to die in such a storm.

Meditation on Living in the Desert

I love the sand, the heat, the arid nights.

I am in love with plants that can survive the droughts.

I am also in love with air-conditioning.

I refuse to recycle.

I am helping to make the entire world into a desert.

I live in the desert. I want everyone else to live in one, too.

When all the trees have disappeared, we can all read Robert Frost poems

and feel sad.

A Good Man Is Hard to Find

"People are certainly not nice like they used to be."

FLANNERY O'CONNOR

This year   the flowers for the dead

are for the man   I found in my yard

on the last day   of September

who was wearing   a silk shirt

yellow   as the walls

of my kitchen   who reeked

of a week's worth   of Chivas

never trust   a man

who reinvents   himself

by drinking scotch   he wants everything

to go down   smooth

as if life   was a new slide

at a city park   on the first day

of spring   maybe

he slid   into the next world

clutching   that empty bottle

in his fist   as if it was the collar

of a priest

his last confession

to shake

the final words

Go and sin no more

was nothing more

who'd cheated him

after putting

into the slot

he can take

with him

depths of hell

take the good

leaving the bottle

not a drop left

and I know

he never

as tight as he clutched

not a cheap drunk

clean nails

a month's rent

brushed wool

five thousand dollars

hearing

clutching, trying

loose

of absolution

as if the priest

than a machine

out of a coke

his last dollar

well, now

his sins

to the lower

but did he have to

booze with him too

empty

for the thirsty

in my depths

held a woman

that empty bottle

give him that

and shoes that cost

good suit too

who had

in his pocket

all in hundreds   plus a twenty

and four ones   and so what if

I took a thousand   or two

before I called   the authorities

he was dead   and had no

use for money   and if he was so loved

and had heirs   in need

of a father's   inheritance

why was he there   dead

alone   in the yard

of a seventy-two-year-old   woman

and why   shouldn't I take

a little something   for the fright

he'd given me   when I stepped out

to sweep   the front porch

him sprawled out   like *my* yard

was *his*   for the taking

and me   a diabetic

with high   blood pressure

I was sorry   I hadn't taken it all

who would know   except for God

and He is as suspicious   of the rich

as I am   nobody reads the beatitudes

anymore and wasn't it enough

that I'd loved men like him

all my life and all I had

to show for it was this house

on San Antonio Street full of moldy

books and wood floors

that creaked with the weight

of all the ghosts that walk to and fro

all night screaming out reminders

that suffering is eternal

and wasn't it enough that I spent

some of the little time I have left

on this once good earth

and a few of his own dollars

for an altar in his honor

him who didn't believe

in the Day of the Dead

until the day he died

marigolds and a bottle of Chivas

right next to the photograph

I'd taken of him as he lay

dead on my geraniums.

Meditation on Living in the Desert

NO. 3

There is a gray bird smaller than a pigeon but bigger than a sparrow nesting in a tree in my backyard. I don't know what kind of bird it is. Denise Levertov would chastise me for my laziness and remind me that a poet's job was to know the names of all things.

Even though I don't know what kind of bird is sitting on the nest, I *do* know the name of the tree: sweet acacia. Its formal name is *Vachellia farnesiana*. (There, Denise, are you happy now?)

A sweet acacia is a desert tree that has thousands of thorns.

The nest the bird has made is made of the thorny twigs of the tree she has chosen for laying her eggs. The bird is unbothered by the thorns. She is content to sit on the eggs she has laid.

Every day I go out to see if she is still there.

I pretend not to see her as she sits perfectly still.

She pretends not to see me, either.

I am playing a game. The bird is not.

I Approach Mr. Max about Visiting Bigger Thomas in Jail

Max discouraged me.
Fifty-two-year-old Mexicans addicted to reading don't know
Two cents about young black men who are pissed off
At the spinning world. (It's true, the world *is* a fucking
Dryer—and *you are* only a rag.) I looked at Mr. Max,
And I could almost see words in those gray eyes—not
That he was opposed to actually speaking. What he said:
"Do you really think that's the best use of your time?"
Mr. Max, he's something. I like him. Not your typical
Slumlord. I looked at him and said, "Max, you think
Defending an inarticulate boy on the verge of manhood
And who says more with his eyes than his mouth and who
Killed a white girl—then killed his girlfriend—is the best
Use of *your* time?" He didn't say *fuck you*. Max, he doesn't talk
Like that. He's serious-minded and civilized. "I wouldn't call
Bigger Thomas inarticulate. Not the word I'd use." He
Smiled. Mr. Max, he has a nice smile. He's always been
Able to afford good dentists. "We all gotta do what
We all gotta do." Mr. Max, he didn't grow up saying
"Gotta," but he says the word like a real native.

Max, he just keeps looking
At me, waiting for me to speak. "Well, maybe I know
A little something about rage," I said, "and I want
To compare notes." Max laughed. "Compare notes? Look,"
He said, "you're not a killer." I looked straight at him
And said, "How do you know?" Max didn't flinch. "I know."
"No, you don't. We're all killers. We just pretend we're not.
You're saying Bigger's an animal and I'm not. That
He's dangerous and I'm not. Hell, Max, we're all dangerous.
We're meaner than Bigger—because, honest to our Jewish
And Catholic Gods, Max, the Gods we can't help
But believe in, well, look, Max, *we are fucking meaner than Bigger.*
We pretend Western Civilization is the title of a play.

16

We're only bit players, but, damnit to hell, let's be honest—
We'd do anything for a chance to stand on the stage.
We've learned our lines and we play our parts, spit out lines
Convincingly. We have clothes for every occasion.
We know exactly what to wear and what to say. That's what
We're good at. Hell, you know that. Pretending. It's all
Such good theater. The performance is what gets us
Through the day. The performance, Max, it's become so real
That we've built the world on it. The whole beautiful lie
Is the foundation of everything we build, baby." Max smiled
At the word *baby* but he let me go on with my little speech.
Yes sir, Mr. Max is a real gentleman. That's a fact.

                                       I smile before I keep at it.
"Yes sir, Mr. Max, you and I, we're killers, too. Killers who
Wear sport coats and read books, collect art and read
Newspapers and magazines. That's not just an opinion—
It's a conclusion to a lifetime of research in the field.
C'mon, Max, let's you and me go and talk to the elephant
That's sitting in our living room, pour him a cup of coffee
And have a real conversation, men to elephant. Max, you
And I are a helluva lot more deranged than Bigger Thomas.
You and I, we're the guys in charge, the guys who make
The rules, believe in them, live our waking days by them.
Max, we set our watches to rules and then pretend
We're free. Well, in the scheme of things, maybe
We are free (let's not think about that too long). But
What about Bigger? What about the desperate poor
Who'll do anything to be able to read the magazines
We get every month. Hell, fuck the magazines,
They'd give anything for the money to buy our leather chairs.
Hell, Max, you know all this in the deepest part of you—
That knowledge sometimes stops you dead in your tracks
As you walk down the street. That knowledge wakes you
In the middle of the night and you swear you can feel
The wet blood on your hands. Lady Macbeth, Max, she's our

17

Patron saint. Yup, we pretend civilization, don't we, Max?
High Tea and Genocide—isn't that the way we've
Always done things?"

          "Look," Max said, "I don't disagree
With your basic message. And I would add that neither you
Nor I understand what it's like to be hated like Bigger's
Been hated. Neither you nor I understand what that hate
Did to him—the myriad of ways that hate—" "Our hate," I
Interrupted. "Yes, yes, our hate," he nodded, "that our hate
Twisted and turned him into a ticking bomb." "Yes," I said,
"We did that." "Yes, we did," Max said. "But it's no use
To see him. Look, I know you mean well, but he's not
An animal in a zoo. You don't know him. Leave him be."
And then he shook his head. "Not a pretty thing, I'll tell
You that. And what would you tell him, anyway?" "I haven't
Gotten that far," I said. "I'm a writer—a real one. Not
Like those hacks typing words for the newspaper—" "A real
Writer," Max says interrupting me. "And I suppose you want
To get at the real story." "Yes. Why not?" "Save your breath.
Save His. We'll find him guilty. We'll kill him. He killed.
We'll even the score. We'll feel better. Nothing will change.
The hate remains. You know this already. You know the real
Story. We all know the real story. Go home, poet. Go home
And do your job."

          My job? The problem is
That my job is not an easy matter. I see myself telling him *you*
Think writing a poem is an easy matter? I see him shaking his head
And saying *you couldn't tell the difference between an editorial*
And a legal brief. But, look, Max is right. I don't know anything
About being hated like Bigger was hated. What do I know?
What was it like, to be a black man in 1940s America? What
Is it like—for that matter—to be a black man in 2007?
Do you know what it means to miss New Orleans? Oh, there's that

Song inside all of us. Yeah, I know. Just like Mr. Max said. I know the real story. We all do.

Meditation on Living in the Desert

NO. 4

Water and trees exist only in your dreams.
Your dreams will not save you from the sun.

Your dreams will not save you from the sun.

Knowledge: The Hand of Another

*He knows that in spite of all the stout talk
of his fellows he must live and die in
uncertainty, a thing blown by the winds, a
thing destined like corn to wilt in the sun.*

SHERWOOD ANDERSON

In the winter light, books open—
Pages, words becoming shadows, the room
Growing darker, sober, sadder, a dark and tragic
Stage. Caesar, Iago, Brutus, Lear perform
Soliloquies, still lifes of murderous
Intents, distilled for years in vats of seductive
Fermenting iambics—words, sentences, nouns,
Pronouns, verbs—and how is it that we
Learn to put letters, words together,
Organize them as if with that alone
We could rearrange the sad and tired
Universe? As if with words alone we could
Undo the damage we have inflicted
With our guns that are more beloved
Than the sincere and saccharine tears
We shed at the first note of "The Star-
Spangled Banner" before the pitcher throws
Out his first slider. If we can alphabetize
A library, why not the gardens and rooms
We inhabit? Why not the stars? Why not
The scattered peoples of the earth?
I would one day like to alphabetize
The emotional lives of my brothers and sisters—
And for one blessèd moment believe
That order is more than a myth invented
By an eighth-century priest with too much
Time on his hands. A cloud is passing. I am

Watching the cloud as I stare out
The window. A passing cloud is a fiction,
A lazy and cheap description of what is actually
Happening. Scientists are clearer, more
Disciplined about these matters. The dog
Is barking. I speak to her as if she were
Human, not knowing or caring what
Words mean to her. What can words mean
To a dog? There is the possibility
Her intelligence may be less questionable
Than the complex and confusing formulas
Of scientists and tragic Shakespearean characters.
The dog, at least, does not put her faith
In linguistic or mathematical equations. Her
Vocabulary is small and pragmatic: *bone,*
Walk, sit. What is language? What is
Knowledge? I know people who claim to know
How to measure intelligence—a misguided
Way to rank human beings as if they were
Ivy League universities. I don't know anyone
Who has ever claimed to know how to measure
A human heart. I know people who understand
Politics and God and the deeper subliminal messages
Of movies and the semiotics of the covers
Of all the books on the *New York Times* Best Sellers
Lists. Perhaps you *can* tell a book by its cover.
Mrs. Skuba, my fifth-grade teacher, would die
If she read what I just wrote. She would sit me
Down in the back of the classroom, force me to
Meditate on what I've become. I'm happy
I became anything. My life could have been
Much worse. And anyway, I'm certain that
Mrs. Skuba is dead, so what does it matter? Other
Things killed her. Certainly not these words.

*

I know people who can tell
The future or the pain of your past
Just by looking at all the lines
In the palms of your hands.
The human hand is a book
Where suffering
Is written in wordless lines.

Tell me again
About the necessity of language.

*

I am thinking of George Willard, how he left
Winesburg, Ohio. I am wondering how many
Scars he took with him and wonder if Salinger
Wasn't right, after all, when one of the heroes
In one of his books said that he had scars
On his hands from touching the people
He loved. I am thinking of Wing Biddlebaum,
How the rumors of a town kept him
From touching anyone ever again, spending
All his time trying to hide those things
At the ends of his arms he once used
For touching. I am thinking of how Wing
Might have been guilty of all the things
The people of the town thought in their small
And ungenerous minds, how he might have been
A saint, a greater mystic than Saint John of the Cross.

*

My wife breathes softly next to me. I wake, get up,
Let the dog out, drink a glass of water, go back
To bed. I look at my hand and think it a strange

Thing, each finger like a separate word that refuses
To be a part of the same sentence. The stars
Are out, sleepwalking in the darkness of the night.
I make my way back to bed—and for a brief
Second, I touch the hand of my sleeping
Wife. The stars have ceased from their nightly
Wanderings. The moon is waning. The night
Is quiet. I fall asleep. When I wake, her hand is still
There. Like corn, I will wilt in the sun. I do not need
To live forever.

                       Her hand. There are moments
When everything is perfect and lyrical.
I know all I need to know.

Meditation on Living in the Desert

NO. 5

Wallace Stevens's blackbirds come into my yard sometimes. I'm not sure
why they like my yard. I suspect they like my sprinklers
and the fact that I don't have a cat.

Even though the blackbirds have learned to live
in the desert, they have never acquired a taste for modernist poems.

What to Do with Lenin's Body

Eighty years   of lying

in public   decomposing

relic in a glass box

his face   in   eternal repose

just like the body

of Teresa of Avila   (how dare

you raise the comparison!

listen! what gives you

the right!)

eighty years

he looks back at us

Lenin!

mirror   of history

let him rest

throw him

in the garbage

leave him

where he is

Lenin   killer of czars

             assassin of the church

             savior of the nation

mind of the revolution

father of Stalin   the butcher

goddamn Stalin the butcher! Lenin

we have you to thank

Lenin! Lenin!

move him

that monster

let him be

let him lie

there in the open

we can walk by

and spit, spit

let us kneel   in gratitude

spit

worship him

no, move him, his mother

waits in a cemetery

in St. Petersburg

blessèd be the womb

that bore him   she

has waited long enough

for her son

such a good

student   of Marx! of Marx!

spit

not Leningrad anymore

ha! St. Petersburg

again   the czars   spit

will have

their pound of flesh   spit

if we wait   spit

another twenty years   spit

will be Leningrad

once more   spit   history

is a circle

round as the earth

round and round

as the clock that keeps

time to the passing

centuries   tick-tock

this is the only music

we know   tick-tock

(the music

of the Rolling Stones

is as irrelevant as

the words

of *Das Kapital*)

tick-tock tick-tock

all arguments

are circuitous

round and round

tick-tock   no one ever really

travels anywhere

round and round   I am

waiting   for

the Cold War

to return—it's just

around the corner

vultures are circling

over the same

damned and rotting

corpse

don't think

your turn won't come

Lenin!

how dare you

blame him

for Stalin

spit   *Lenin*

people are singing

your name

they are fighting over you

like jealous lovers

bury him deep

until anyone who

remembers his name

who loves him   hates him

is dead

no more resurrections

for that bastard

democracy

is a beautiful thing

the American presidents have

done wondrous things

see and believe!

thank God

Communism is as dead

as Jerry Falwell

(do you know what I'd

like to do with *his* body?)

Lenin! Lenin!

he was a saint, I tell you

do not bury him, do not

toss his body out

into the open air

hell! hell! hell!

let the nation

smell smell smell

the stench

ahh, he's dead

dead   spit

this is what remains

a corpse   that refuses

to decay   a public

argument   that will

never   go away

(wait around, baby

this argument will soon

turn into another war)

you want a definition

of history? We are condemned

to argue about

what to do with—

Lenin!   *Listen!*

I could never grow

a goatee and can't decide

whether I loved

or hated you

Meditation on Living in the Desert

NO. 6

The mesquite growing outside the window where I write

is in full bloom, its branches swaying in the breeze.

By August, the pods will hang heavy and fall

to the ground. When I was a boy I used to chew

on the pods pretending they were sugarcane. Maybe only boys do

such things. This summer, I am contemplating

a return to my old boyhood habit of chewing

on the pods. This will give me an excuse to spit

when I am reading the *New York Times Book Review*.

The Philosophy of Work

I

         It's one of those things—you're walking along
And out of nowhere you remember a dream: your younger
Brother José is telling you that he just doesn't give a damn
About books—and though he doesn't say it, he thinks whatever
It is you do, well it sure as hell isn't work. Your brother goes
Around the country retrofitting smelters and refineries. *Now that's*
Work. In the dream, your brother has a sneer on his face. You wake
Angry at your brother and then remember all the cruel things
Your brothers—all of them—did to you when you were small
And defenseless. And then you lecture yourself: *Look, you can't*
Go around holding people accountable for the things they say in your dreams.
This is not about your younger brother. It's *your* dream, not his.
One summer, when you were going through lonely adolescence,
You and your brothers, Ricardo, Jaime, and José, worked
Picking onions alongside your father. You would all rise early,
And you—*you*—would ache for another hour of sleep, sit in
An angry silence in your corner of the pickup truck
As you massaged your own tired muscles and cursed the world
Of work. You can still smell the heat of the soil as it baked
In the sun, the onions lying on the ground like corpses
After a battle. You can still smell your brothers' sweat
And the rancid odor of yellow onions that filled the air
That summer when you were fourteen. You still remember
Swearing that the books you read would save your life from this,
From all this work. Even now, when you are at a grocery store,
Selecting just the right onion, you wonder if the pay has risen
From twenty-five cents a sack. You know exactly how
You feel about the minimum wage.

2

The words *class* and *work* are as real to you
As the Bazooka chewing gum you got for free when you got
Your haircuts at the barbershop on Picacho Street. Work
Is a sore subject in your house during the summer. Your wife
Is good-naturedly jealous of the life of a professor (though,
To be honest, you had more invested in your identity as a smoker
Than in your identity as a "professor"). What is it about
The word *professor* that makes people want to hit you? All
Your attorney friends hate you. They call you up, friendly, ask
You what you're doing. You tell them you're reading a book.
A book! Hell! *Reading a book!* They're ready to call the D.A.
And have you indicted—hoping you just might need
A good attorney. Reading a book in the middle of the day.
Explain that to a judge. Look, if they're all so busy
Working, why the hell are they making phone calls to poets
In the middle of a summer afternoon? "Listen," you say,
"You want to trade salaries?" You very much enjoy
The silence on the other end of the phone.

Yeah, everyone likes a good punch line—
Even lawyers and professors. A few years back, an old friend
Said you should do stand-up. Making people laugh for a living—
That sounds glamorous. But sitting around writing jokes all day?
That would be a lot of work. You'd rather write novels and poems
About work. After years of thinking about this, you have
Finally arrived at the insight that life can't be just about work.
But the truth is that everyone *is* always working. *I was going up*
For the weekend but something came up at work / Sorry, Ma, I've been
So busy at work / Honey, look, I know I said I'd be home by seven
Never trust anyone who can't talk about anything except work.

3

You remember your other younger brother telling you
That the goddamned Communists have taken over America,
"Can't fucking smoke anywhere anymore, and they're always
Watching to make sure you don't drive around drunk."
You're wondering why he thinks driving around drunk
Is such a good idea. "Look," you say to your brother, "you're full
Of shit. You wouldn't know a Communist from a Republican."
You feel a little bad for saying that because you understand
That everyone has to get their politics from somewhere.
You understand all too well that your brother has acquired
His politics from a watering hole overflowing with the talk
Of a bunch of guys who reek of sweat and cigarettes and beer,
Guys who would rather go straight to a bar after work
Than go home to attend to whatever's waiting for them there.
Home isn't a holy word for everyone. You understand this.
And then you see the condemning look on your brother's face,
The look that said, *Sellout*. In Spanish, the word is *vendido*.
In either language, it is not something you want to be. You
Get that look sometimes. Yeah, sure, *vendido*. In your opinion,
The word is greatly overused, tossed around too often
And too vaguely. Whom exactly did you sell out to?
For what? For personal or political gain? Maybe
You missed something. If you sold out, you should have asked
For more money. Instead you asked for summers off.
You're not complaining. Yeah, sure, you're not complaining.

4

Sometimes, you watch the dog
Taking a nap and you are utterly in awe of the absolute sincerity
Of dogs. You enjoy studying the way they stretch and don't feel
Guilty about anything. They would never make good Catholics.
And they don't like to work, either. You wonder if watching dogs
Qualifies as work. Your wife works hard. She's like her mother.

She has a work ethic that would put any good Lutheran to shame.
Come to think about it, Protestants have nothing on Catholics
When it comes to work—look at all those Mexicans flooding
Into our country. They cross thousands of miles, go through
Unbelievable contortions, get cursed and slandered by right-wing
Talking heads just for a chance to work. You wonder what it's like
To be white and enraged at poor Mexicans—those fucking
Lawbreakers who are illiterate and come here half dead
With nothing but the word *work* in their strong and stubborn hearts.
You wonder what it's like to hate some of the poorest people
On the face of this sad, post–9/11 earth. You wonder what
It would be like to be them, to be the vessel that holds
All of your country's hate. Which brings you back to the issue
Of the minimum wage and child labor laws and the politics
Of picking onions. You start getting the feeling that everything
Is connected but you just don't understand how. You tell yourself
That before you die you want to become a mathematician.

5

                              Your sister works at a bakery.
She entered the workforce at seventeen and she has never
Had one damn summer off. Not ever. Over all these years of being
Gainfully employed, she's learned the meaning of gender
Discrimination firsthand and stood up to more than her share
Of managers who took better care of their ties than they took care
Of their female employees. You are in love with the stories
She tells: *I told that sonofabitch that he didn't know cream cheese frosting*
From sour cream. All these years she's placed her body at risk,
Walking in and out of freezers, burning her arms and hands
In the oven. All those scars and then losing her sense of time,
Rising at two in the morning. Your nephew, your sister's son, wants
To work at something that pays more money.
                              Who wants to be poor?

Your father worked his ass off. He died poor.
His children paid for his funeral. So maybe that made him
Not so poor: having daughters and sons to pay for his funeral,
That's a good deal. But having sons and daughters is another kind
Of work. I watch young parents at the park, chasing down
Their children as they kick and scream bloody murder. You say
To yourself: *Looks like work to me.* You see old men working outside
In other people's yards. You have the urge to ask them how much
They make. That's not cool, asking people how much they make.
It's like asking people how old they are. Not cool. It took you
Seven years to write your first novel. Writing a novel is a lot of work.
A kind of work you didn't know how to do. You had to learn.
Learning something—that's a lot of work, too. You love to say that
To your students. They don't believe you. They give each other
Knowing looks. Some of them roll their eyes. They prefer to believe
In "talent." They prefer to believe that some people are born
With a "gift." They want you to point and say things like, "You!
You there! You have a real gift!" They don't like hearing the word
Work on the lips of a writer. If they wanted to hear that word,
They could stay home and listen to lectures from their fathers.
You like to work out in the yard. You hate to work out at the gym.
If you have the time to work out at the gym, then maybe you don't
Work very hard. Your father belonged to a union with hundreds
Of other working men. Getting your politics from a union
Is better than getting your politics at a bar—or even from
Hanging out with your friends as you're sailing on a yacht. Neither
Your brothers nor any of the guys that belonged to the union
Ever set foot on a yacht. They never worked out at a gym
A day in their lives. Your grandfather taught you that a real man
Knew how to work. You don't know if he meant working
With your body or working with your mind. You're still working
That out. People in America work hard for what they have.
Just ask them. Rich people do a different kind of work
Than poor people do. That's a fact.

6

Years ago, at a party, someone asked you what you did
For a living. *Write*, you said. You remember that look
Of condescension, that look that said, *In other words your wife*
Supports you. Look, writing a poem or a novel isn't exactly like digging
A ditch. And it isn't like defending an innocent client, either. No one
Understands the value of what you do. Not even you. Now
When you go to a party, you tell people that you are a professor
At the university. Not even that convinces them that you work
For a living. Certainly not your brother. Everyone in the world
Is obsessed with work. *And what do you do?* My students are too busy
Working to pick up a book. When you give them assignments,
They get this look on their faces. They are trying to tell you
That you are giving them too much work. Sometimes, at the end
Of the day, you get really tired. You're tired of thinking. Thinking
Is a kind of work. A kind of work that's really hard. People should
Do more of that. They should do it every day. Maybe living
Is nothing more than work. Sometimes, in the back of your mind,
You keep hearing, *Work makes freedom work makes freedom work—*

Meditation on Living in the Desert

NO. 7

In summer, you have to rise at dawn. Before it gets too hot.
In winter, you may rise from your bed anytime you please—though
this may disqualify you from earning a living wage.
Even people who live in the desert have to work.

I never met a Mexican who had the time to lean on a cactus.

The Comforts of the Neighborhood

in memory of Juan Patricio

Sand. The sky. Litter on the pavement: wrapping
from a Payday, a cigarette butt, a crushed cup

from Sonic: America's Drive-In, a note on lined paper
from a neighborhood boy to a neighborhood girl,

I think I'm crazy for you. Do you think you could be crazy for me
too? Will you meet me in the park? Would you let me kiss you?

The remains of a careless civilization. Water running
down the asphalt street. An old woman shaking

and shaking her head, watering the street in the heat,
such a waste, a sin, all this, and where is a vengeful

God when you need Him? A wild cat clawing
a plastic bag full of rotting scraps. Another cat

on the hunt, lying in wait as birds circle and land,
circle and land. The transplanted palm tree—two

years and still struggling to stay alive like an exile
living in a country that will never love him,

a refugee repeating the same simple question every
day of its miserable life: *Why am I condemned to grow*

roots in a land not my own? And houses. Everywhere
houses, well-kept, made of stone and brick and built

to last. And you tell yourself that on the inside
these houses are immaculate and full of objects

collected on trips to foreign countries—Mexico, France,
Japan—every cherished item in its proper place. And

houses that want for care, houses whose paint has
faded and peeled in the heat of an unforgiving

sun. And houses recently renovated and whose fresh
paint shouts out the owners' newly acquired taste

for color. Ahhh! And you find yourself shaking
your head and you chastise yourself for your

shallow and banal thoughts because you know
that this does not matter, that none of this matters

as you think of the bones of the dead women
of Juárez and you wonder who is killing them—

after all this time, they do not know and you have
told yourself a hundred times that they do not know

because they do not want to know because these
women do not, did not matter and you think of that

young man, nineteen, Juan Patricio, shot by agents,
surrounded in a sea of uniforms in his final

moments, and you see him as he lies in the street
and you remember the altar, a cross, candles, flowers,

his name on the sidewalk, *this, this is where he was
killed.* You do not want to think about these things

and so you continue to scan the houses on your morning
walk, houses that are beginning to fall into despair

and hopelessness because the owners can no longer
maintain order and have given themselves over

to the chaos of weeds that threaten to swallow up
not only the yard but the entire house and its tired

inhabitants. And you know the chaos inside must
be even darker and sadder, and the tears in that

place are like the waters of the deep after God
flooded the wounded world and put it out of its sinful

misery in a single vengeful act of kindness (the first
recorded case of euthanasia). And other houses, just

a spit away, large and prosperous and tasteful, filling
your head with the wonders of capitalism. You think

of that postcard you saw once in a book, that
postcard with a white man in a suit and his blond

wife, and his blond children and wwii airplanes
flying overhead and at their feet, the motto:

To protect our way of life. And you wonder why this un-
welcome thought enters you and owns you for a brief

and violent moment until finally the airplanes and the man
in the suit and his family are gone and you shrug

your shoulders, and turn away from the houses, the houses
you see every day, and you turn your attention to the gray

sidewalks. Sidewalks you trample on every morning. Poured
cement, a path on which to walk—and you see lawns that are

perfect, manicured, fawned over like spoiled children.
And neighboring lawns that have rebelled against

the whole domestic landscape, lawns that not so subtly
inform you that they are sick and tired of being trained

to make the earth look tame as an English garden
because this is not England and high tea is as foreign

a phenomenon here as blowfish for dinner. And despite
the fact that this part of the world has been colonized

several times over, it is still not and never will be
tame—and it is blasphemy to pretend otherwise. And

people rushing out to their cars, their thoughts already
on the work they must do to keep the house they have

just locked with a key. And their dogs, barking and begging
for one last touch from the lord of the house who

is leaving again. Every day. Always leaving. What remains
is the innocence of dogs, these dogs who are unable to

understand the reasons for all these comings
and goings. Innocents. Pets. Condemned to look out

from behind the fences where they are kept, longing to
roam the streets—and be a part of the world they see

every day. And an old man is telling an old woman
what he has been hearing about, all that awful bombing

in Iraq and wasn't it all terrible, and she nodding and saying
yes, yes, isn't it all the most terrible thing, all those young men

dying and young women too, and well, this just isn't like
fighting Hitler, now is it? And I've changed political parties

despite the fact that I will always love Ike and Mamie. The dogs
are barking. I am breaking out into a sweat in the heat

of the day and all I can see is a young man, nineteen,
Juan Patricio, his heart pounding as he hears the explosion

of a gun being fired. He is falling on the asphalt. The Saturday
morning is perfect and calm. The Border Patrol agents

are hovering around him. Confused moths fluttering
around the light.

                              No one says a word.

Meditation on Living in the Desert

NO. 8

Do not attempt to cross the desert on foot.
This is serious business.
Ask any Mexican.
If you don't trust Mexicans, ask
any Border Patrol officer—though some of them
are Mexican, too.

Prayer in the Garden

Today, he will not bend to pull a weed. He does
not labor in the garden. He sits in the coolness
of the morning, feels the grass on his bare feet,
waits for the sun to rise, wandering through
the yard, touching plants and humming
an old Mexican song, the one his mother liked
to sing when she was washing clothes. He remembers
winter, how he'd look out the window and wonder
at the starkness of the leafless world. He is grateful
for the summer, for the green of the fine and tender
leaves of the mesquite. He is grateful for the thorns
of the paloverdes in bloom. The season will not—

Nothing is forever, not this garden, not his life,
not the slant of light that falls on the face of his wife.

The Book of Eschatologies

...and the sea was no more.

Prayer in the Garden

The heat has come to the desert
almost as punishment. As he gives water to the thirsty
plants, a grasshopper, the first of the season.
He thinks of the plagues of locusts in the Book
of Exodus. He thinks he remembers that locusts
also hovered over the Book of Revelation like
avenging angels—though in this he may be mistaken.
But he is not mistaken about the violence
of retribution. He remembers dissecting large
grasshoppers in his biology class in high school.
He remembers the clinical smell of formaldehyde
and how his grandmother's lilac perfume could not
hide that same smell when he saw her body
at the funeral home. She died in 1969, two years
after the Summer of Love. Flower children
and Haight-Ashbury were not in her vocabulary.
Mostly, in that last year of her life, there was only
room enough for phrases like *no aguanto el dolor.*
The cancer that had tortured and taken
his grandmother was dead, too. He guessed
that the only way to kill cancer was to die. But what
was the great sin for this death sentence? So what
if his grandmother liked to cuss. She liked to laugh
and kiss, too. He remembers the smell of dead frogs.
He remembers writing his reports late into the night.
He wonders what became of that black book
with his name written across the front of it like ashes
on the foreheads of repentant Catholics.

As he digs his fingers
into the soil, he has the urge to grab a fistful
of earth and rub it into his skin.

The Ruined Cities of My Broken, Broken Heart

I

      The still streets glowed
in the dark
    as if the sun
were buried just beneath the asphalt
     where it was about
     to break free

     from the surface
where it had been carelessly
discarded.
          Night had come
to the city

     deciding to stay forever.

2

      You missed the sun.
That is what you remember most
about the dream,

how you missed the sun
     like a lover waiting
at the window for a return
    come back come back
in the beating
     of your panicked heart,

how you missed the sun
in the same way you missed your niece,
your dad, your grandmothers,
your boyhood dog,

missed the sun
in that deep and painful way
that makes the insides
                of an old slave
moan a grief far beyond

the shallowness of tears.

3

        You knew the light
would never come again.

4

        Slowly you stir,
wake to your simple rituals, alarm
clocks, the news on the radio,
morning rites of reaching out
to touch the woman, the man,
the familiar body, a finger
running over
the childhood scar—

5

        So many things
would never come again. Not
the busy streets filled with the lovely
and pedestrian concerns of the minds
and feet and shoes that cluttered the sidewalk
like confetti in a parade. Parades!
Parades were gone! Imagine a world
without parades and political signs
that spelled out beautiful things
like *Peace* and *Blessèd are the poor*

and *No more war. Never again war.*
So many beautiful and dazzling things
in the world that had been

and were no longer.

6

Every night the dream.
Every dawn, the waking
to that profound
state of sadness and solitude.
Always you rushed out
into the yard and wept
at the sight of the honeysuckles in bloom
and the blueness of the sky.
Imagine
a world without the sweetness of jasmine
and honeysuckles? Imagine a world
without the perfect breeze,
without the perfect blue
that only a sky in June can give?

7

Imagine the whole world a desert.

8

You remember now.
The dream was the same, the city dead,
in ruins, empty. A different city
in each dream. Sometimes the city
was El Paso. Sometimes the city
was San Francisco. Once, the city
was New York. Another time

it was Denver. And then, in succession,
Los Angeles, Chicago, Paris,
London, Iowa City.
Lafayette, Las Cruces, Leuven.

You spent your youth living
a nomadic existence.

You moved from
one place to another. Each place, each
city, a different

season in your life.

Imagine all the old seasons gone,

leaving only an eternal age

of dark and sunless days.

9

Once, your heart was a desert.

10

As Mexicans would have it:

Cada cabeza es un mundo.

Every single mind
constitutes a world—

an ecosystem.

Each life

a city

      with streets, avenues,
      libraries, histories,
      museums, homes,
      gardens, alleys filled
      with garbage, kitchens,
      aromas, secrets,
      and novels that contain

      voices that must not

      become extinct.

I I

Pearl Harbor

Here and there,
a whisper
a question
a finger pointing at the sea.
The sounds
of clicking cameras.
A graying man
is crying as he reads
the names
of the dead
on the white marble.
      Women are taking
off their leis. They are throwing
their white orchids
on the waters that float
over the rusty body
of the *Arizona*.

 The flowers float out
into the harbor and disappear.

Amid the silence and the grace
of orchids on the water
the eternal questions shove
themselves down our
unsuspecting throats.

There are echoes of the dead
everywhere we turn.

12

You have been wandering
in the desert for forty years
searching for water
and a politics
and a theology
and a city you can call home.

13

Imagine drowning
in the unforgiving waters of war, reaching
for air like plants reaching for light.

14

 The familiar aroma
of fresh coffee, the headlines,
something—every day,
    something bad
    something good
minds awake, wandering, mulling over
yesterday's agendas *God, you forgot, oh shit*

the schedules, the newness,
the oldness, the sameness, maybe
this will be the day,
the day you have been waiting for
all your life, such a lovely—maybe—

15

Imagine living in a world of eternal shadows.

The world of eternal shadows reminds you
of Plato. When you were eighteen

you thought Plato was a protofascist.

Franco must have read him just before

                he had Lorca killed.

16

You've lived long enough now

to love what you have lost.

You have to be careful.

You don't want to live

in the past. You have said this

a thousand times:

You detest nostalgia.

17

Death makes preservationists of us all.

18

The plants in your house bend
their leaves toward the window
searching for the sun. The word
for this phenomenon is *phototaxis*.

19

Sometimes, you wake in the night.
You are afraid. You are afraid
that your heart will become
                a desert again. Uninhabitable.

20

                The smell of the city,
the feel of the concrete, the newly washed
streets. *The newly washed streets.* This is the day
you have been waiting for all your life.

21

                Close your eyes. Picture
the clouds in an August sky. Describe
the smell of gardenias and creosote
to a four-year-old. When you wake
in the dark, picture the light
                                in the room.

This room is the world you live in.

22

You are trying to remember the name
of the cultural anthropologist
who said we yearn most for the things
we kill: birds, elephants, trees. Oceans,
soldiers, American Indians.
Imperialist Nostalgia Yesterday
the words popped into your head
when you heard a story on the radio
about the politics of ivory. You dreamed
elephants attacking the city in which
you live, reducing everything to ruins.

You do not blame the elephants.
Vengeance has an impeccable logic.

23

        The word *fuck* is unlyrical
and obscene. Such a word does not
belong in a poem. (Among
other things, it lacks dignity.
Plato never used the word.)

You prefer civilized words, words
of substance, words like *phototaxis.*

24

The air. The air. The smell of last night's rain.
The faint memory of bruises, hurts, and pain.

A finger runs across a childhood scar
as you find your space and park your polished car.

25

You are closing your eyes.
You are whispering
                all the names
of all the cities
                    you have loved.

26

Jesus went out into the desert to pray.

27

You are trying to separate
the ruins of all these cities
from the shattered
pieces of your broken, broken heart.

*

This is not a dream. The world
you love *is* in ruins. Ask any Iraqi,
he will tell you the truth of it.
What does it matter what word
you toss out into the empty world?
Fuck? Phototaxis? Love?

28

The world you live in is gone.
There is nothing you can do to bring it back.

This is what war has always done.

29

Like everyone else before you

you have wandered into the desert
          and been tempted by the Father of Lies.

30

You have lived
through *obscene*
and called it duty.

You have lived
through *obscene*
and called it patriotism.

You have lived
through *obscene*
and called it civilization.

Let's all say *fuck* together.

31

You must go out into the desert again.
You must live there in silence
until you encounter God.

32

If you were like your plants

—phototactic—

then your only concern

would be stretching
toward the sun.

33

You see yourself walking on the perfect
lawn, graves all around you,
in the valley of the ancient crater
of an extinct volcano. Eight hundred
graves are marked *unknown*. As you walk
along the silent rows, you read names
and dates, add up the numbers
in your head. *This one was nineteen,*
this one was twenty-two, this one was
twenty-four. And this one here, he
was thirty-five—

34

If you were like your plants?

35

Imagine being buried
in a grave marked *unknown*.

Let us all give in to nostalgia.
Let us go and pray.

　　　Let us all kneel
at the marbled altars
where we have sacrificed
the perfect bodies of boys
to the insatiable gods of war.

36

They tested the bomb
in the desert—
then named it Trinity Site.
What did those men
see in the light
of that new sun?

37

This year, an infestation of locusts.

38

Trinity Site. Is this a theology?

39

The fall of Tenochtitlán
must have felt like the eschaton.

It *was* the eschaton.

*

Hiroshima. Nagasaki.
Maybe that was the eschaton, too.

*

You have heard people yearn for
the days of Masses in Latin,
days when *that* classical language

was the lingua franca
of the civilized world.

*

You think your theology doesn't have a politics?

*

Fuck nostalgia.

*

You have always wondered
how many languages were spoken
in the Americas before
Europeans imported
English and French
and Spanish and Portuguese.

What if the earth
is sad and broken
and cannot keep living
without the sound
of all those languages?

*

      Someday
in the desert, you will build a
New Jerusalem.
      The tired sun
will be new again.
      Your dreams
will no longer be of darkness.

The city will be
teeming with all the peoples
of the earth

and they will all be legal.

Is this theological nostalgia?

40

Let's all go out to the desert.

Let's all say *fuck* together.

Let's all say *hurt* together.

Let's all say *no* together.

Let's all say *yes* together.

We will gather in a place
they call Trinity Site.

Together in the desert.

Together we will
all say *peace, paz, pacem.*

Prayer in the Garden

It's true, he was once deeply in love
with Ash Wednesdays. He became addicted to
repeating *Remember that you are dust and to dust you
will return.* He became obsessed with trying to
decipher what T.S. Eliot had to say about
the subject *Because I do not hope to turn* He remembers
being sorry for everything, for spitting on his brother,
for wanting to be an only child when he was five, for
stealing eggs from chickens, for hating Ernie Valles,
for holding anger in his head as if it were a special
knowledge, for desiring material things he could not
have and did not need, for slamming shut the gates,
not letting anybody enter his own private property,
a No Trespassing sign posted deep in the corners
of his young and stubborn body. His selfishness
must have surely angered God. The wind
kicks up, a storm coming, and suddenly
he is surrounded by the yellow blooms the wind
is tearing away from the paloverde. It is snowing
yellow blossoms.
                          He lifts up his arms
and smiles. *Sursum corda sursum corda.*
The grasshopper leaps away as he senses
                                        the thunder

                and then the rain. Like the heat,
the angry drops fall to the thirsty earth with a savage
                    and unmistakable rage.

The Book of What Remains

You are what you remember.

Meditation on Living in the Desert

Always carry water. This, too, is serious business.

After the Dying

for Brian

My life is not. The way it used to be. When I walk, I no longer
look down at the ground. I am no longer at one with things
that crawl. Now, my eyes are curious and searching—
not that I know what I'm searching for. I've always been afraid.
I've always been unsure. So I closed my fists tight around the word
certainty. I thought that word would save me, make me happy.
Now, the word is gone. Do you know how much it hurts
to let go of the word I thought would save me?

*

My life is not what it was. I don't look down at the ground.
I am in love with the color of the sky.
        Staring at the blue. That's my new addiction.

*

    Today, I was walking down a clean and strange sidewalk
in a city where I do not live. I don't live anywhere. Not anymore.
I'm redefining home. *Home* is related to *certainty.* The rain was soft,
a tune was turning in my head. Did you know there were songs
inside of me? I should have known that. Why didn't I know?
I hate myself for not knowing. I hate myself for hating myself.

*

    I passed a man on the sidewalk. He was walking
in the opposite direction. His eyes met mine for an eternal second—
and then he smiled. I smiled back. There was nothing unusual
about this subtle exchange. It happens every day. We could have

averted our eyes, looked away from each other, been embarrassed—
but what did either of us have to be embarrassed about?

                                       That man, he reminded me. Of you.
I think it was the eyes. Or just the way he carried himself,
the way he stopped to tie his shoe. He was laughing at himself.
I thought of the look on your face. I can't ever think of you
without thinking of that place. There are so many people
in the room. All those faces entering my head. Do you see them, too?
Their eyes keep staring into mine. I can't turn away so I just let them
enter as if my brain had become a living room: *Come in! Sit down,*
sit down! I went through a list in my head and put the names
to all the faces. I smiled. I still remembered. All the names
and all the faces. And all the fucking stories, our sad and tattered
histories. There are certain things I won't forget. Forgetting
is a kind of death. I'm done with all that dying.

                 *

                        I think about that lonely place. It's always
with me now. When I was there, each day I'd wake and ask
Why, God, am I here? I don't belong. Exhausted, I wanted to run.
Running in my days, and in my nights, and in my dreams.
Learning to stop. It hurts like hell. I had no idea I'd carried
so many goddamned tears. I had no idea how much they weighed.
But there was no pushing the tears and dreams away. I used to lie
awake at night and think *how strange, how very strange. I've died and gone to hell.*
I felt myself on fire. The wounds opened up like a burning sky
and almost swallowed me whole. Hurt is a monster, a garden
that needs tending. *Take care of the monster. Or the monster will take care of you.*

                        After the dying, I wanted to live.
In order to live, I needed to go to the place of the pain. The place
of the pain. One night I dreamed I was crawling through that desert.
I kept whispering *water.* I thought of Jesus. I thought of Him: *I thirst.*
Thirsty men fall in love with thirsty gods. I remember whispering

I have to leave, I have to leave right now. I almost packed my bags
and left. Running is the greatest addiction of all. I yearned
for my old life and for certainty. And for home—

but home had disappeared.

*

Have you ever felt your heart hurt so much

that you just wanted to fucking rip it out?

Every day I woke to find myself still there—me
and my struggling hurt. Why was I still there? Why hadn't I disappeared?
Goddamnit, goddamnit, I hate this, I hate this, I hate this.

After the dying, I wanted to die.

*

A few weeks after I'd left that place, I had a dream. I'd gone back
and I was walking the lonely labyrinth, the ground covered in a blanket
of snow. I was walking barefoot, impervious to the cold, naked
and perfect. I was five the last time my body had come in contact
with that word. My feet against the snow made me feel alive. Alive
is a place. *Alive* is the new word for *home*. I was laughing—even now,
weeks later, I can hear the laughter of that dream. I felt as brilliant
as the morning sun, and as I reached the center
of the labyrinth, everyone was there.

Everyone. You, too. You

were there. And *all* the pain was gone.

You should have seen the smiles, the looks in their eyes.
Their brokenness had made them saints.

When I woke, I wanted to cry. Tears don't always mean hurt.
Tears don't always mean grief or sorrow or pain. Sometimes
tears just mean   you're alive.   I wanted to cry.

*

I wonder how many of us made it. I wonder how many of us
finally managed to unlock the door and step out of our dark
and sunless rooms. Sometimes I want to call you on the phone
and shout: *Tell me that we are all alive. Tell me that we have all been saved.*
Tell me our eyes are all turned toward the sky. You can't. You can't tell me
that. I know you can't.

My memory will return me there, return me
to their faces, to the sounds of their voices, to the echoes
of their pain. My body is scratched with names.
I don't know how to live without the scars.

Tell me I can keep their names.

*

There is a scene that hangs on the wall of my memory
as if it were a fresco in a church: you are sitting in a chair
in a small office cluttered with childlike drawings.
I am standing in front of you. I am struggling to say
something I've never said. *Not even to myself.*
I am looking down at the ground. Your eyes
are blue as the sky. Your eyes are speaking my name.

When a man takes out the words
he has hidden in his heart for over fifty years
and gives them to another—

that is called a miracle.

Meditation on Living in the Desert

NO. 10

If you do not stay out of arroyos during a thunderstorm,
you will drown. People will laugh at your funeral and snicker,
He drowned in the desert. If you are strict
about keeping this rule, when the time comes for you
to die, you will more than likely have a dignified funeral.

Meditations on Music, Joseph McCarthy, and My Grandfather

(WITH FOOTNOTES)

> *We will not walk in fear, one of another.*
> *We will not be driven by fear into an age of*
> *unreason, if we dig deep in our history and*
> *our doctrine, and remember that we are not*
> *descended from fearful men.*

EDWARD R. MURROW

     Sin música no hay vida.[1] My grandfather used to say that
Every few months, to remind me what was important—
And to remind himself, too, I think. Mostly we talk to ourselves
Except that we need someone else in the room so it will seem
As though we're having a conversation instead of a monologue.
Enrique has a theory about how people communicate.
According to him, most people aren't interested in listening.
They just smile, pretend good manners, and wait
For you to stop talking—at which point they jump in
And have their say. All anyone ever does is wait his turn. Life
Needs music in order to keep us entertained as we patiently wait
For the attention to turn to us so we can open our mouths
And spit out whatever it is we want to spit out. Speaking. Waiting.
Life. Music. *Sin música no hay vida.* There's an impeccable logic
To this kind of thinking. Who wants to live without music?
No music equals no dancing. No dancing equals no sex. No
Sex equals no—you see exactly where I'm going with this.
Let's face it, I've heard some crappy songs in my day.
Let's not name names. Joseph McCarthy ruined it for everyone,
That sonofabitch.[2] Was it the booze, I wonder, that made him

---

1. *Without music there is no life* (an old Mexican saying).
2. As it happens, Senator McCarthy was censured by the Senate the same year
   I was born. Life does have its own kind of symmetry.

So mean? If you drink enough booze for a long enough period
Of time, you begin to see all kinds of crap: Communists,
Cockroaches, turtles speeding down the freeway. Some people see
Monsters, Democrats, the devil. Did you ever see that old
Ray Milland movie *The Lost Weekend*? Alcohol could do bad shit
To you, that was true enough. Back in the day when I partied
Too hard, I never saw anything extraordinary. I never
Had a *Reefer Madness* moment.[3] I knew that you could have
Reefer Madness moments when you'd had too much alcohol—
I saw it happen, guys going crazy and blacking out. But nothing
Like that ever happened to me. Mostly I slurred my words,
Got a little sleepy—although I have to confess that, as dawn
Was approaching, some of the guys standing around
Started to look like El Greco painted them—
Which is not necessarily a bad thing. Who wouldn't want
To have hands like El Greco's Saint Andrew? He had hands
A jazz pianist would envy.

                    Not every drunk is mean.
But one thing I've learned: *all drunks think they can sing.*[4]
Why is that? Even my father hummed to himself when
He was drunk. That was a long time ago. When he got sober,
The songs on his lips dried up and wilted. His brother,
My uncle Willie, liked to whistle. I thought he was at least
As good as a bird—though I'm no expert. The fact that
My uncle Willie whistled all the time didn't mean
He was happy. He was happy only when he was drunk. My mom
Used to sing as she worked. *Now, she was happy.* There is no
Logic to this. She worked and worked and worked. And yet,
There she was: singing and listening to those old Mexican songs
On the radio. I have no explanation for her kind of happiness.

---

3. We used to go to the drive-in movies all the time, and we saw that movie several
   times. My friends and I, we thought it was the best comedy ever made. It made
   everyone I knew want to smoke marijuana.
4. While the Irish prefer the sentimental "Danny Boy," Mexicans usually wind up
   singing the equally sentimental "Volver, Volver."

When I work, I never sing. I just don't. Work, to me
That means writing. The thing about writing is that it's always
Your turn to speak. It's like being the birthday boy who gets
All the presents at the party. It's *his* birthday and it's his
One chance to ignore the looks on the other kids' faces,
The looks that say: *We think you should share.* No, I don't sing.
But sometimes I wake up with a really dumb song
In my head and it sits there all day, nesting like a bird waiting
For her eggs to hatch. I mean dumb songs like *I'd like to buy*
The world a Coke. Who wants to carry *that* song around all day?
I don't even like Coke.[5] What's a song, anyway? Do we
Really need to drag out the *OED*? When I was sixteen
My father proclaimed that the music I listened to was nothing
More than noise. He was no fan of Grand Funk Railroad
Or the Doors. He didn't get what the hell was going on
In the music of Iron Butterfly. He said they all sounded
Like they were all high on marijuana, which is another way
Of saying that they were all having *Reefer Madness* moments.
Look, just because they were high doesn't mean their music
Is bad. I think I knew what my father was getting at:
Not every voice is worth listening to. Let's not name names.
I really do hate Joseph McCarthy. You think hating him
Does any good? Hating him is like my uncle Willie's whistling—
It doesn't make you happy.

                    Birds in the morning,
That's a kind of music. I'm not British. (Who would want
To be? So what if I did love the Beatles.) Still, the word *lovely*
Comes to mind when I hear birds singing outside my window
As I wake. They're talking, actually, not singing, trying
To survive, but hell, they sound better than a lot of stuff
That's out there. I'm surprised they haven't cut a record deal.
What I really like is jazz, especially old songs: "The Haunted Heart"

---

5. The truth is, I used to be a serious coke-aholic, drinking about ten cokes a day.
   I've long since kicked the habit and have been unable to touch soft drinks since.
   Coffee is another matter.

Or anything on the lips of Nina Simone, songs that should
Make you sad but don't because they're simply exposing
The lyrical side of pain. You can't live without pain.
That would be like living without music.

      My grandfather grew sweeter and sweeter as he aged.
If you asked him how he was doing, he would say: *Encantado*
De haber nacido.[6] I know that my grandfather wasn't always
An old man—but I know next to nothing about his youth,
Except that he was addicted to hopping trains and liked playing
The guitar. By the time I came along, he'd given up his youthful
Pastimes in favor of gardening. Some said his gardening
Was a kind of music. I never really cared for the music of the hoe.
Once I saw him strumming a guitar, his worn fingers thin
And gnarly.[7] There was a grace in my grandfather's hands
That astonished me. This was something of a miracle—
In my twenties *nothing* astonished me. He did, he *did*
Look like one of El Greco's paintings. If Joseph McCarthy
Had hopped trains and played the guitar as a young man
And had grandsons who were content just to watch his hands,
He might have fallen in love with music and might not
Have needed alcohol to silence all those demons
That were screaming in his head.[8] We might have been spared
That mean-spirited moment in our nation's history.[9]
There might have been another jazz era and no McCarthy era.
We might all have gone around saying: *Encantado de haber nacido.*

---

6. In English, the phrase roughly translates into: *Enchanted to have been born.* It
   doesn't sound musical in English—in fact it sounds overly formal and preten-
   tious. But in Spanish, it's a very beautiful thing to say.
7. The guitar in question was actually mine. It made him happy to think that I was
   learning to play the guitar. He gave me a rattlesnake's tail to put in the guitar.
   He said that the rattler of the snake would make the guitar sound better. Frankly,
   the guitar would have sounded better had it been in the hands of a more gifted
   musician.

As history played itself out, Joseph McCarthy became
A drunk. As I said, all drunks think they can sing. That's the rule.
For every rule, there's an exception. Joseph McCarthy
Was the exception. If only he'd known that music was going
To outlive the Communists.

       If only he'd had a song inside him.

for Enrique Moreno

---

8. I don't know if McCarthy ever had a *Reefer Madness* moment, nor do I know if
   he was touched by Ray Milland's performance in *The Lost Weekend*. I do know
   that McCarthy died of cirrhosis of the liver in 1957.
9. McCarthy's approval ratings a month before he was censured stood at 35 per-
   cent. George W. Bush's approval ratings when he left office stood at 23 percent.
   Like a good many people in this country, I am obsessed with polls though I don't
   always know what they mean, although I have some serious educated theories.
   My serious educated theories coupled with my left-leaning ideologies will more
   than likely be the subject of another poem.

Meditation on Living in the Desert

I am looking at a book of photographs.
The photographs document the exodus of Mexicans crossing the desert.
I am staring at the face of a woman who is more a girl than a woman.
She is handing her documents to a government official.

I know and you know and we all know that the documents are forged.
The official is not in the photograph.

Only the frightened eyes of a girl.

How in the Night (and the Meaning of Your Life)

1

How, when you wake in the night, the civilized world asleep,
And nothing else awake but creatures of the dark who are not,
In all probability, monsters but certainly phantoms, unfriendly, angry
Rats clawing and gnawing, *rats I tell you!* rats that have managed
To make a home in your head and perhaps your heart too
As if your entire self were nothing more than an abandoned
Sewer line just waiting to be colonized by *rats I tell you!*
And how, as you lie awake, you sense their intimate—if unwelcome—
Disquieting presence, and you fight the urge to make the sign
Of the cross and call an exorcist or an exterminator, but
It is two o'clock in the morning and no one will come.

2

You are left there in your own private archipelago of terror
So your only escape is to focus on the sound of the distant train
But there is no sound that can distract you from the thoughts
That are attacking you *rats I tell you!* and you understand
That you are not only a stranger to yourself but a stranger
To the world you inhabit, a visitor, a foreigner, an illegal.
Who let you in? Who in the hell let you in—you
And your infestation of rats? You remember the young woman
In San Diego who, years ago, handed you a note. *Why don't you
Go back to Mexico?* You wonder what it all means, to be
A citizen? To be alive? And you begin to question the value
Of your life and you think of how it all ended for your father
And wonder how it will end with your mother and your brothers
And your sisters who smoke too much and don't want to quit
And how it will end with your ex-mother-in-law and your ex-wife
And for the world that is choking on the crap we toss out
Onto the ground, and into the oceans *did you know we are killing*

All the fish? and into the sky that will never be pure again, and how
We refuse to clean up after ourselves because it really *is*
Too inconvenient *It's the economy, stupid!* too inconvenient
And overwhelming, so instead you turn your attention
To a respectful and tasteful formal poem that meditates
On a medieval painting of a Madonna and child—surely
That will save us. Well, at least console us. And how you wish
To hell that you could get rid of that painful fragment
Of Eden before the fall (*before the rats*) that is lodged inside
Of you like an inoperable tumor and you wonder
Who in the hell thought it was a good idea to plant
Biblical stories in your boyhood head that made you
Believe and yearn for something pure but you don't want
To think about these things and certainly you
Don't want to meditate on your life and what it's worth—
What is that, anyway? Your life isn't a leather jacket
On sale at Macy's. You can't put a price on the fifty-four years
                    You've spent and misspent on the earth.

3

You begin making a list of all the things you did not do
In the house you no longer live in, the weeds in the yard,
The pink Formica on the countertops that will forever
Point a condemning finger at your failure to re-do the kitchen,
Your failure to banish the fifties from your house, the roof
On the garage that was about to collapse, and you wonder
Why you cannot get that house out of your head because it was
Only a house and you no longer live there, so you begin
To make another list of things you did not do, a list
That has nothing to do with that house, that idea for a painting
That tugs at you and will not leave you in peace and the canvas
Still unstretched, the unwritten letters of recommendation,
The unread papers of your students, alone and ungraded
In a stack on your desk, the unfinished pieces of writing
That are scattered about your office and everything in the job

That is your life seems to be like broken pieces of a Grecian urn
And you whisper with the desperation of a dog, wounded
And whining, "If only that urn were whole again." If only. Then
You would be able to see the truth of who you are, you
In all your beauty—but that is not possible so you have
To settle for the fragments that have been given to you. But

Then, the moment of panic leaves you. And how you smile
And breathe in and out, breathe in and out, relax
Because the meaning of life is not to be found in moments
Of insomnia and insanity. *Never mind about the rats* yes you smile
And promise yourself that in the morning, you will wake—

4

How you will wake and read a book by García Márquez,
Something beautiful and true, yes that story where

Florentino Ariza and Fermina Daza are finally united

      After fifty-three years, seven months, and eleven days
And nights of yearning.
            And how, as you read, you might find
The meaning of your life.
            Ah, love, let us be true to one another—
The meaning, the meaning of your life.

Meditation on Living in the Desert

NO. 12

We are killing the river.
The rains are disappearing.
We are building houses where there is no water.
I am staring at the wall we have built.
If you stand right next to the wall you will feel like you are in prison.

You are in prison.

Let's all say *fuck* together.

Arriving at the Heart of Tragedy

No med'cine in the world can do thee good.

LAERTES

There are certain things that cannot be
Undone. Lot's wife glanced back at Sodom as she was
Fleeing—and just like *that* she became a pillar of salt.
Who knows, maybe she adored her beloved city
More than life itself and only wanted to say *adiós.*
Maybe she was thinking, *I can't believe that God is doing this.*
Or maybe she wanted to see if she could escape
With one little transgression in her pocket—
Like cheating on your diet. I wonder if she had time
To curse herself for her arrogant stupidity or curse God
For being such a stickler? *Him and his fastidious conditions*
For salvation. I wonder if there was one last moment
Of terror and wonder, too, how one last moment of terror
Would feel. Lightning and thunder in the heart.
That's what I think. One of my ex-wife's ancestors lost
Everything—his cows, his horses, his barn, his house,
His property. Everything lost in a lousy game of poker.
What in the hell was he thinking? I picture him walking
Home, grumbling at his great misfortune, shaking
His head, cursing his life and wondering what words
To use when he made the sad and solemn announcement
To his wife, *Corazón, I have lost everything we ever*
Worked for. Would he add: *I had a full house, a good hand*
But—I think he must have talked himself into believing
That it was meant to be, that it was fate, that it was all
A part of a grand scheme—that he was nothing more
Than heaven's pawn. He kept his wife's glare in the darkest
Corner of his heart till the day he died. He would never
Be sure if she had truly forgiven him. You can't take back
A poker hand. Another thing you can't take back: the words

You speak. Everyone knows that. Somehow it doesn't stop us
From saying inane, insipid, hurtful things. Family courts
Are teeming with women and men who couldn't take
Back all the mean things they said to one another.
At a certain point *I'm sorry* becomes a hollow phrase. *I want*
A divorce. You can't take back those words.

Hell, you just drown in them.

*

The whole world is littered
With what-ifs. What if Eve hadn't tasted of the fruit
Of the tree of knowledge. If she hadn't done that,
Then everyone would adore snakes and none of us would
Have to work. Imagine, hanging around naked all day, not
Having to go to work. You know, if we had to hang around
Naked all day, maybe we would take better care of our bodies
Instead of covering them up with designer clothes. No
Work would mean we wouldn't have to worry
About illegal immigration (and we would have to invent
Another reason to hate poor Mexicans). What if Othello
Hadn't believed that low-life, manipulative, lying bastard,
Iago? He and Desdemona would have had a nice life
And beautiful biracial children. What if Orpheus
Had not doubted, had not looked back to make sure
Eurydice was following him out of the underworld? If
Only he hadn't doubted. Instead, his promise broken,
Eurydice descended back to live at the side of Hades
And Persephone, and he, Orpheus, drowned himself.
All that work for nothing. Sometimes, I think we look
For ways to be unhappy. And more than that, we want
To elevate our unhappiness into the realm of tragedy
As if we were all auditioning for a leading role
With the Royal Shakespeare Company. But why
Does everything have to be so tragic? Who can stand
To watch the dysfunction of the Macbeths? It's all

Such a bloody mess and what's so original about
Ambition? And what if La Llorona hadn't drowned
Her children in the river? What story would we tell
To scare our children into behaving? And what
Kind of solution was this, anyway? See, Mexicans
Are like the English: they are in love with tragedy.
Only Mexicans take their tragedy home every night—
The English leave it at the theater.
        All of this has something to do
With Catholicism and Protestantism and history.

                       *

                I hide keys in the garage
So I don't have to worry when I lock myself out.
I have spare glasses everywhere so that I will always
Be able to see. I have more than taken Elizabeth
Bishop's advice to lose something every day. But
None of this qualifies as tragedy.
                I keep thinking of the man
Who forgot his infant child in the car as he rushed off
To work. He was in a hurry, running late, preoccupied.
His wife called in the middle of the afternoon, wanting
To know why their son was not at day care. In a panic,
He rushed out of the building. I keep seeing this man
As he reaches the place where he parked the car, knowing
That the heat of the day must have—*no, please, God, how
Could I have forgotten, no, God, no* I see him as he flings
Open the back door to the car. He is inconsolable
As he holds his limp son in his arms. *How could I have
Done this? What have I done? What have I done?*

                       *

Many years ago, my ex-wife gave me
A sculpture as a gift: Quetzalcoatl is lying down
In a small and lonely boat. He is in mourning.
He, too, is inconsolable. Tenochtitlán has been razed
To the ground. Cortés has won the day. Quetzalcoatl alone
Has escaped to tell the others: *Mexico has fallen.* He is
Floating out to sea, holding in his hands an image of a world
With a cross firmly planted into its core.
        The Christianized world has arrived
With an army that cannot be turned back. The Aztec
World has been destroyed by fire. For Tenochtitlán
There will be no resurrections—and for Quetzalcoatl
There is only this eternal and solitary travel in a sea
Of endless sorrows. I try to imagine what it is like to feel
The weight of that kind of grief. Lightning and thunder
In the heart. I keep seeing the man, a dead son
In his arms *why should a dog, a horse, a rat, have life,*
And thou no breath at all? The world is in ruins.
We are left cursing and clutching at our bitter hearts,
Wondering, wondering why we are not dead.

Meditation on Living in the Desert

NO. 13

I am remembering the first book of poems I wrote.
That was a long time ago.
I used to know what poetry was, what it did, how
it was written. I wrote something about the Navajo,
how eight thousand starving souls

were forced to cross the desert on foot.

Human history is even crueler than the desert.

Translating the Universe, or Morning of the Lunar Eclipse

I

                         The eyes' translations are immediate.
I have never known how to scientifically explain a lunar eclipse.
Explanations—scientific or otherwise—are not the same
Thing as experience. Death is a perfect example. Some people
Are in love with explanations. Others with experience. I don't know
Anyone who's in love with death—not even believers
In the resurrection of the body. When I was a boy, I was
A student of the sky. As I progressed at school, it became obvious
I would never become a scientist. This fact broke no one's heart.
A broken heart has no scientific explanation. Despite
My unscientific bent, somehow I would know a lunar eclipse
If I saw one. To hell with the translation. I've known her
Since I was sixteen. *Her.* Ginny. Have you ever had a friend
Whom you've known for over thirty-five years? Do you know
How many conversations and glasses of wine that translates into?
She never forgets my birthday, calls me every year, always
In the morning, tells me she's happy I was born. There is something
Untranslatably sweet in this simple gesture that has become
A yearly ritual. The translator is reading in Portuguese. The sound
Of that unknown language does not remind me of Portugal
Or Brazil. Instead the sound reminds me of Latin, how,
At the age of five, I could catch a word here and there,
How sometimes I knew exactly what was being said, and then,
The next moment, I would be lost in a forest of language.

2

                         Getting lost in that forest of language can be a terrifying thing.
It's something like a moment of insanity. Have you ever experienced
A moment of insanity? Getting lost in a desert is even worse.
That's more like a moment of death. I don't want to die of thirst

In a desert, longing for a destination that is itself a lie. They are looking
For a soldier in the desert. The soldier is nineteen and he is just back
From the war in Iraq. He has gone AWOL and looks very much
Like a boy in the photograph that appears in the morning paper.
I get a long message on my cell phone and it's *her*, Ginny (and no
It's not my birthday), and she's thanking me for referring her sister
To an acupuncturist—an acupuncturist with magic hands
Who has learned to listen to animals as they talk back.
He understands everything his cats say to him. Imagine not
Having to guess at what animals are thinking. There are, of course,
Times when my dog makes herself perfectly clear. I am listening
To the translator's English translations. The poems sound plain
And dull and I wonder what has happened to those Portuguese poems
I thought were so ineffable? Perhaps nothing is ineffable. Perhaps
That word corresponds only to an impossible human need. We are
All so greedy. There are soldiers, hundreds of them, searching
The desert for the young private who has gone AWOL. Someone
Must have seen him wander off into the desert, taking his arms
With him as if he were going off to war again. There are people
All over the world who are clamoring for the Mass to be said
In Latin. You know, like back in the fifties. Everything was better
Back then. Just ask any black man who was in his prime
In that blessèd era that has become the focal point of our nostalgia
As if the whole decade were nothing more than reruns
Of *Father Knows Best*. There were only eight lynchings
In America in the 1950s. In the 1930s there were hundreds.
Evolution. We practically lived in Paradise. I think there are millions
Of Catholics who have talked themselves into believing
That Latin is a holy language. Everything sounds better
When you don't know what the hell is being said. Unless you suffer
From paranoia—in which case you believe you are being
Talked about or stalked by everyone around you, no matter
The language. This is like believing that you are guilty of all sins.
Imagine the penance for that. Imagine that kind of suffering.
I wonder if the lost soldier wandering around in the desert
Is trying to atone for the sins of the world. Maybe just his own.

No one knows what goes through a mind in turmoil. What
Scientist can tell you that? Who can understand the terrors
Of an unforgiving heart—especially if that heart is your own?
And what is the word *sin* attempting to communicate? How
Does that word translate into a human life? We all have conflicting
Theories about this. We call those theories *theology*. Is the word
Peccato substantially different than its English translation?
Please let's not get into transubstantiation. I can't take this.

3

                                     It's a very sad condition
To suffer from, paranoia. Ever listen in on a cab driver, talking
On his cell as he weaves in and out of traffic in Manhattan?
I'm always grateful I don't know what's being said. I am sure,
Perfectly sure he is not talking about me. I'm just another tourist
From Texas. When I was young, I occasionally smoked pot.
When I engaged in this illegal activity, I did it casually, and I
Became one of the happiest guys in the world. I loved everyone—
Even people I didn't like. I had a friend who stopped smoking
Marijuana because he got tired of thinking people were trying
To hurt him. I suppose you could say, our bodies translated marijuana
In divergent and opposing manners. How many meanings
Do you think the word *marijuana* conjures? Ginny's voice is alive
Inside my cell phone. When you've been hearing a voice
For thirty-five years, you don't need a translator. She is telling me
That her sister has three herniated cervical disks (I had four
But this isn't a contest). If everything in life is a contest
And if you absolutely *have to be* the smartest person in the room,
Please go to an expert on mental health. This disease is progressive.
Progressive is not always a good word—not even in the lexicon
Of unreconstructed leftist intellectuals. The translator is explaining
Her theory of translation. I am no longer so sure I believe
In translations but I very much doubt that we can live
Without theories. Okay, we can't live without translations, either.

Will someone please translate George Bush for me? Ginny says
The acupuncturist helped her sister in just the right way. She loved
Him. The way she says *loved him* makes me understand the gravity
Of the situation. But right in the middle of the conversation
(Even though I wasn't actually on the other end of the phone),
She says, "Jesus, a car just hit another car—right on the freeway.
Jesus." And then she pauses and loses all her words for an instant.
What happens in the brain when you lose all your words?
They have found the young soldier. He was no longer alive
When they reached him. He took aim at himself with
His military-issue rifle. There are many theories as to why
This young man decided to end his own life. Do you see
What I mean when I say we cannot possibly live without theories?
We would have no scientists without them and the word *gossip*
Would disappear from our vocabularies.

4

                              My father had no brain activity
When we took him off the respirator. I thought it was a blessing
That he was, at last, free of words. The translator is reading
Another poem. Portuguese is flowing from her mouth. The words
Are like rare orchids leaping from her tongue. Her body is like
A garden. I remember the old priest. He was kind in the confessional.
I don't believe he ever understood a word I said. Latin flowed
From his mouth in the same way that Portuguese is flowing
From the mouth of the translator. No, not exactly. Latin
On the tongue of a priest always made me feel accused. We don't say
Mea culpa and beat our chests for nothing. Once, on Christmas Eve,
A man who made his home on the street came into the sacristy
And grabbed a young priest by the collar and spat into his face:
"What has your fucking Jesus ever done for me?" Good question.
"Jesus," Ginny says again. I think of how I would pronounce
The son of God's name in Latin. On my clumsy lips, it always
Came out in Spanish. To tell you the truth, sometimes even my English

Comes out in Spanish. Even now. I am my own worst translator.
Just ask my students who are always asking:

>   *What in the hell is he talking about?*

5

           I am listening to Ginny's silence. I am thinking
That there must be a scientific name for those moments when
We lose the ability to speak. I think of Zachariah, how God
Struck him dumb because he didn't believe. A man named
Gustavo Villoldo who was once a CIA operative is planning
To auction off a lock of Che Guevara's hair. Am I alone in thinking
That this man is a lunatic? He is also the proud owner of a map
That was used to hunt down Mr. Guevara in Bolivia, and he possesses
Various photos of his dead body. I wonder if the authorities found
It necessary to photograph the dead body of the soldier lying
In the desert. I see Ginny as she is driving down the freeway talking
To me about the transformation of her sister's back since her session
With the acupuncturist and how she is thinking about making
An appointment with the acupuncturist, too, because—God knows—
She has ailments. Anyone who's over fifty has ailments. And this
Just from listening to talk radio. People on talk radio are trying
To translate the world for you. They're lousy at it. Some people know
Only one language. These people are perfectly happy in their self-contained
And monolingual worlds. The things other people say in other
Languages don't matter a damn. They don't have to worry about
Having useless dialogues that end in wars anyway. What difference
Does it make what someone else is saying?

6

                         Maybe it's not so bad
To be autistic. Is it better to be autistic or paranoid? Those are
My choices? I know an older woman who hates Mexicans
Because they don't know English. (And she doesn't believe
They know how to take baths.) She still mourns the death

Of the Latin Mass even though she thinks it's okay to shoot
Mexicans in the back if they're trying to get here illegally.
There are senators and congressmen who agree with her.
I wonder how many of our immigrant relatives simply overstayed
Their visas? Remember this: you may be the child of an illegal.
Relax. Smoke some marijuana. Sometimes I think Catholicism
Is more a mental illness than it is a religion. Me, I think
We should show more discernment when we apply
The death penalty. Latin. Some languages refuse to die.
Even languages that are dead.

7

                              In the days before mass media
There had to be proof that a traitor or an enemy of the king
Was dead. That's why they placed their lopped-off heads in public places.
Thomas More comes to mind. *See, he's really good and dead.*
Everyone got the message. The English were particularly fond
Of this tradition. Tell me again they're a subtle people.
When the camera came into existence, photographing dead criminals
And leftist revolutionaries became a high art. The translator
Is telling a story of how she arrived at the Portuguese poet's door.
The first thing she said was that she was really hungry.
The poet fed her. The mouth, too, can translate as immediately
As the eye. When it's not busy with words, it can taste. I have never
Been able to describe the taste of Oaxacan *mole*. Taste is untranslatable.
Have you ever listened to wine experts describing the taste of wine?
Which would you rather do—listen or taste?

8

                              I find myself wondering who
Is going to bid on Che Guevara's lock of hair. Some wealthy
Conservative still gloating about the defeat of leftist revolutionaries
Who'll take it out at a party when all his guests are drunk *we got*
The sonofabitch. That crowd, no doubt, will be delighted. That's my theory.

I used to sign in at the Hoover Institution and read the *Daily Worker*.
I was looking for poems. You think life makes sense? I just saw
A documentary about a young man, not yet twenty. He was from
A small village in Mexico. You know this story. He stopped
And asked an old woman for a drink of water. No one can live
Without water. That's not just some theory. The woman's husband
Chased him down with a rifle, then shot him in the back of his thigh
As he ran. He and his wife waited for hours as they watched him
Bleed to death. I think a part of me would like to own an original
Photograph of Che Guevara's dead body. The other part of me
Thinks that the part of me who would buy a photograph of a dead
Revolutionary should be committed. One less lunatic walking
The streets. The voice of an old friend on the telephone is a language
All its own. When my wife was trying to tell me something,
I didn't need anyone to translate. I understood her perfectly—
Even when I was pretending I didn't. I know a young woman who believes
She has had AIDS and has been cured of it. She says she is exhausted
From all the vaccinations. She hears voices. For all any one of us knows,
Teresa of Avila and John of the Cross heard the same voices.
Maybe one of those voices whispered the theory of relativity
Into Einstein's ear. I have never understood mysticism. I've never
Understood physics, either. The lady on the next block swears
The chief of police is watching her. She is collecting crabapples
From my neighbor's sidewalk and talking to herself. The people
Of Juárez who work in the maquilas make under fifty dollars a week.
This is legal and sane and part of a perfectly respectable
Economic system in which we all participate. Somehow, we believe
Going to Mass will save us from all this.

9

        Who in this room is in favor of bringing back
The Mass in Latin? Raise your hands. I chastise myself
For not having returned Ginny's phone call. I promise myself
I will call her tomorrow. It is 4:45 in the morning. I wake
From a dream. In the dream, my father is in a nursing home

And I am visiting him and he is begging me to take him back home.
My mother is also in the dream and she, too, is begging me.
When I wake I can't remember what my mother was asking
Of me. The dog is pacing back and forth in the room. I hear her
As she walks down the hall—then walks back into the room,
Stopping at the side of the bed as if summoning me.
She doesn't growl or bark or speak. She wants something.
I am trying to guess. I am not my acupuncturist and I have never
Heard voices—but what do you call writing a poem? I don't know
What my dog is trying to say to me. I think of the translator,
The priest, Portuguese, Latin. I have known my dog for thirteen
Years. She is an old friend and I know her well enough to know
That she is waiting for me to get up and follow her. I rise, place
My feet on the floor. The dog walks toward the French doors
That lead to the backyard. I follow her, open the door, and we
Step out into the dark. She lies down in the middle of the yard—
Then looks up and sniffs the air. I, too, look up and I am a boy
Again, a student of the sky.

                        I have woken from a bad dream.
I have let my silent dog lead me into the backyard. I am standing
In my underwear. The breeze is cool. I am staring at the darkening moon.
I think I could stand here forever. It is almost five o'clock in the morning.
At this very moment I have no need of a translator. I, who am in love
With theories, have no need of a theory. I am watching my dog
Lying on the grass. She is quiet and at peace.
                    I am lost in the full eclipse of the moon.

Meditation on Living in the Desert

Jesus spent his entire life living in the desert.
This is why he is not bothered by the impure language
and the impure thoughts and the impure people
that inhabit the border.

He knows what it has cost us to survive.

Last Summer in the Garden

...and dust you shall eat all the days of your life.

I

I am walking toward a garden that was once *my* garden.
I have been away. Too long. I have lived for the moment of return.
I have been walking for many days and nights, and now it is morning,
And I have finally arrived. I run to the gate and push it open. I am wild
With a joy I have not known in many years. But when I walk
Into the garden, I see that it has become a desert. The plants,
The trees, the shrubs are gone. Everything has become dust,
An empty desert, dry and waterless and dead. I fall to the ground,
My face against the scorching sand.
       I will lie here and die. I will lie here and die.
And then I wake. But the nightmare continues in the waking.

2

I am not the first man to be exiled from a garden. Exile is dirty
Business. Dirty or not it's been going on for centuries. It's a kind
Of insanity to believe that my story is the only one that matters.
When you have the big picture in your head, it's hard to play
The victim. It hurts, that's true enough, and the tears are real, too,
And there is no use in pretending that there are days when your heart
Can hold nothing but your grief. Take a breath. Cry for all you're worth.
But don't forget, everyone else is crying, too. There is plenty
Of misery to go around. Don't let the smiles fool you. We're all living
In exile—it's just that some of us don't know it. You think the guy
On the freeway who's tailgating you and flipping you off isn't
In some serious pain? He wants you off the road, which is
Another way of saying he'd like to exile you from the fucking freeway
Of life. Forgive him. He's only doing what he's been trained to do.
He doesn't know where to put his pain and has mistaken it for rage.

See, that's what we do,
We exile each other. This isn't pretty. And it doesn't feel
Good. When I think about it, my fate is laughable. I am a small
Shack on a dirt road in a small village on the map of the world.
I keep thinking about exile and wondering why it never goes out
Of style. I have a political answer: exile provides a space for opportunists.
That's where capitalism comes in. There is always a way to make
Money. I know a guy who flew to Haiti and sold pencils on the street
Just to make a few bucks on the side. This is a true story. Name me
One contractor, one big farmer who's against hiring Mexicans—papers
Or no papers. Why is that? Because they're progressive humanists?
Because they recently read the beatitudes and were moved to tears?
Who was it that profited from the lands the Japanese had to relinquish
When they were sent to the camps? Exile would be a good name
For the phenomenon of being forced to give up everything you own
And relocated to live in government camps. *Relocation* is another word
For exile. The poor of Mexico are relocating themselves to the United States
Because their own country has no jobs for them. This is a problem
In a country full of hungry people. Will someone please tell
The local parish priest that God is in love with the poor? Okay, so maybe
The rest of us don't give a shit about the beatitudes, but what's *his* excuse?
Yes, I know that priests are busy protecting the rights of the unborn.
But what about the rights of the born? This is not good for my sobriety.
Listen, the poor are dying so they come north. They abandon
Their homes by the millions. We don't call that particular historical
Moment of mass exodus *exile*. Hell, we don't even call it *relocation*.

I have come to the conclusion that God
Writes letters that spell out *exile* on the backs of hungry people.
They'll do anything to get into countries that have trees teeming
With fruit. They're looking for food not knowledge. I know we love
To play God, lying in wait for a chance to catch *those* people
In the part of the garden where they just don't belong. There are
Millions upon millions of voices who could tell you stories
About exile: sad, sad stories that would make you weep. Millions.
From every continent—Africa, Asia, Australia, the Americas.

Adam and Eve, they started a historical and theological trend.
The world has become too enamored of their punishment.

3

I never liked this whole business of blaming Eve for tasting the fruit
From the forbidden tree. You don't have to be a trained psychologist
To see misogyny disguised as faith. Read the story and think about it.
Yes, it's true that the Bible is a long and arduous book badly in need
Of editing, but it is not impossible to understand. I know people
Who think they know what that book says even though they've never
Actually bothered to peruse its pages. And while we're at it, where does
It say "apple" in the text? How is it Eve's fault that the serpent
Seduced her? How is it her fault that she had a curious mind? How
Is it her fault that Adam was a passive idiot? I don't believe in punishing
Eve and her kind—just as I don't believe that all men are idiots. Not
All men. The truth is I'd rather be Eve than Adam—though
That may have something to do with the fact that I overidentify
With women. Maybe that's part of living in exile, the guilt over
Betraying your own gender. I have never felt at home in a men's club
Or in an all-male shower. Not that I don't like being a man.
I confess that I like having a penis—not that I've always
Known what to do with it (pissing doesn't count). My experience
Of being a man has been a little harsh. Rape will do that to a boy.
Trust me when I say that rape is one of the many imaginative forms
Of exile that Western culture has perfected over the years.
As I said: I am not the first man to be exiled from the garden.

4

                                    I have this image of Adam hiding
From God. On fire with his fear, with his shame. I know
What that's like. I've bathed myself in shame for many years. There
Was no cleanliness to be found in those waters. In the theology
That I inherited, there was never any talk of original innocence.
There was only an obsession with original sin.

5

I am remembering how I used to wake in the mornings and step out
Into my backyard, coffee cup in hand. I am remembering how
I would wander around in a sleepy stupor, the cool of the morning grass
On my bare feet, the awe of the new day making me forget about
The word *exile*. I keep dreaming the desert willow, the sweet acacia,
the honey mesquite, the purple sage, the cow's tongue cactus that had
Become as tall as a tree.

                                   God, I loved that garden, but
It's no longer mine. It's not true to say it's gone. It's just that
I can't set foot on it any longer. It's cruel, this business of exile
And divorce. I won't deny it—I have a few things to be sorry for.
I have to pay for my sins. That's the way the game has been played
For hundreds of years. Where do I get off thinking I should be
The exception to the rule? It's no use to cry *No fair.* I may never
Be the man I want to be, but this much is true: I am no longer a boy.
When the umpire cries: "You're outta there, chump!" it's wise
To slink back into the dugout with as little fanfare as possible.

                              I can *never* go back to that house
Where I lived for so many years. That house with a wife and a garden,
That house that held everything a man ever dreamed of having. I was
The god of the garden. I was the planter, the giver and taker of life.
This year, in early June, the front yard was a blanket of orange blossoms
And the paloverdes were exploding in yellow blooms that were
As fragile and tender as my boyhood. I was not there to see the garden
In its fullness, though I saw the entire scene as a photograph
I stole from my memory. I miss the idea of innocence and perfection.
I miss the romance of creation. But it was time to let the old ideas die.
The truth is that there were serpents everywhere. Their whispers
Nearly drove me mad. I had to wake myself. Once I stepped out
Of the dream, there was no path of return.
                         I have spent my last summer in the garden.

Nothing may ever be mine again.
But when we leave the garden, always we carry something with us,
A fragment of our innocent selves. There is a freedom in living
Somewhere east of Eden. We all want to taste the fruit from the tree
Of knowledge. I'm thinking that, in the end, Adam and Eve
Made their peace with exile.
              And I can make my peace with mine.

Meditation on Living in the Desert

On July 16, 1945, they tested the bomb. In the middle of the New
Mexico desert. When I think about that day

I think about religion. I think about science.
I think of rejecting both.

Let's all say *doubt* together.

What I Have to Sing About

for Aaron

Lately, I've been singing. Not in public, *not with this voice*, but singing
In that casual, turn-off-your-brain, private, pedestrian way. It's not as if
I'm imagining an audience. This is not about applause. *This is about something
Called happiness.* How's that for sincerity. Sincerity—it's the new irony.
I've been sincerely and unironically singing my guts out for the past few weeks.
It's almost as if my brain is an iPod full of songs and something about the air
Or the color of the summer sky or the tree teeming with astonishingly green
Leaves or the passionate graffiti on the wall written in bloodred spray paint
Or the I-might-be-in-luck spring in the walk of the person who's hurrying
Down the street or the jazz riff in the person's voice telling me
About something he feels, *something he really feels, something profoundly personal*
Pushes just the right button and a song comes sputtering out of me. Does it
Matter that my song sounds like a lawn mower that's about to give out? Look,
You don't want to hear me sing. Me singing is not a beautiful sight, though
You might get a good laugh at the silly grin that's pasted to my face. So
I have a grin and a head full of prematurely graying hair.

                                        Is that something to sing about?

                    *

                              God, sometimes I wish I were
Juanes or Tom Waits or Bruce Springsteen. Or even Barry Manilow. But
That's a lame regret. I have regrets that are much more real than that. Regrets
That are cut-your-heart-out painful. Painful to the point of paralysis. Many
            years ago,
There was someone I should have kissed and didn't. That *didn't* changed
            my life.
There was someone I *did* kiss and shouldn't have. That *did* changed my life, too.
If ever there was a bad Robert-Frost-road-not-taken moment, well, I won't
Get into it. Regrets can kill a man. Regrets can turn into late-night drinking
            sprees

With no one to keep you company except Billie Holiday's voice singing
"I Cried for You." This is not good. Look, if you don't take regret by the
        throat
And say, *Fuck you! Get the hell out of my house!* then, baby, it's over for you.
The world is littered with bodies killed by that particular bullet. And
        believe me,
That bullet kills so slowly that you'll be dead long before you're dead.
I've given myself some advice: *Say you're sorry, Benjamin. Say you're sorry*
And mean it. And don't expect to be forgiven. Take the slap on the face and
        move on.

*

I've thought about this for a while now and let's just say that the next time
I'm about to kiss or not kiss someone, I'm going to think about it very
        seriously.
Kissing someone at my age is a very serious thing. I've made some wrong
        turns
And gotten lost. I even lost myself. My entire self. If you have ever lost
        yourself,
You know how skyless and starless and dark the world can become. Still, I
        can
Sing about the journey. Why the hell not? Listen, even when you sing the
        blues,
It's singing. Yeah, we're back to Billie Holiday—but this time without
The bourbon. Listen, does it matter that my hurt has haunted me since I was
        five?
Does it matter that I've misspent millions of hours hating myself? I took
The theology of *mea culpa* to new heights. Does it matter that I wanted
To drink myself into the next millennium? Look, no one ever said that
        depressed
People are original. Depressed people are too depressed to use their
        imaginations.
Yeah, a million misspent hours. That's a lot of misspending. I can't resurrect

Those hours. Remembering—that's different than resurrecting. Does it matter
That I am sometimes so riddled with guilt that I feel like Pancho Villa's body
At the very moment of his assassination—riddled with bullets, I tell you.
It's a bloody fucking mess. I've got no one to blame but myself. Blame? Hell,
Let me just walk past that word. It's not a helpful word, not in my opinion.
Trust me, I've been in therapy. I have made that word illegal. And the good
            news
Is that I've never been narcissistic enough to say with anything resembling
Conviction that *everything is my fault*. I'm over the *mea culpa* theology.
It just didn't work for me. Let's face it—I've made a few mistakes. I hurt
Some people. I saw the look on their faces. I've seen the tears of disbelief
And the hurt. I dream them, the people I hurt. I may dream them forever.
But *everything is my fault? Listen, Benjamin, everything is not your fault.*
                    From my perspective, that's something to sing about.

                    *

                                        Things could be worse. I could be
George W. Bush. I could be Dick Cheney. See, I'm grateful for my life already.
Okay, not being someone else? Is that all I've got as a reason for singing? What
Have I got to sing about? Good question. I'm suddenly divorced. I lost the
            house
In the settlement. I lost the dog, too. Have you ever lost a house you loved?
            I planted
All the desert trees and shrubs. I shaped it into my vision of Paradise. Gone.
Lost it. Have you ever lost a dog you named and trained? A dog who loved
Your smell so much that she stole your T-shirts and took them to bed with her?
This is all very sad. My own personal tragedy. No, I am not Prince Hamlet,
But I love that dog and grieve her loss. Go ahead and laugh at my tears
And the whole drama of the man-dog thing. Love is infinite—didn't anybody
Tell you? My love for dogs does not diminish my love for my own kind. And if
You think about it, my dog and I are *real* and Hamlet was just a character in
            a play.
Do you know how many literary critics love that play more than they love
            people?

Do not scoff at my love for my dog. *Do not*. And so what *if Hamlet was*
A very good play? Fuck *Hamlet*. Listen, I dream about that dog just as I dream
About the woman who kept her. I would like to say that I hate the woman
I'm divorcing—for keeping the dog I love. For other reasons too. Except
That somewhere inside me I know the truth of the entire matter. Yes, I know
That no one will believe me when I say that I love the woman I've left. But
This is the good part: *No one has to believe me*. Love and Divorce and the songs
I sing are not things that can be explained. I'm done with explaining.
Yes, *goddamnit*, all of this has something to do with happiness. Maybe
The way *you* love makes sense—but *my* love makes no sense at all.
And neither does my life. Living is not a tragic play. Living is not
A lesson in logic. Soliloquies and syllogisms have never, *not once*,
Helped me solve one fucking problem concerning my relationships with
The people I've loved. Ever try a soliloquy on your mother? Have you?
Ever try to engage her with your impeccable logic? How'd it work out for you?

*

Look, I'm lucky to have walked out of my old address
With my toes and fingers intact—though, frankly, I'm still looking for my balls.
Did I expect to walk out with all the furniture and no hurts, no scratches, no
Scars? I'm fifty-four years old and I'm starting my life over again. Believe me,
The one thing I know how to do is start my life over again. But how many lives
Do I get? At least this time around, I don't have to resort to waiting on tables.
At least I'm not forced to suffer other people's inane conversations
About remodeling the bathroom and maids that don't speak English
For a lousy 15 percent tip. So what exactly *do* I have to sing about? Divorce?
        Divorce
Is not only *not* original but it's nothing to be proud of. A wife who feels
You betrayed her and hates you for destroying her life and hates you even more
For your inability to be a real man is not exactly what I dreamed of putting
On my résumé. Ex-priest, ex-smoker, ex–dog companion, ex-husband.
Rack 'em up and break 'em, boys. Yeah, I feel like a fucking billiard ball.
A few months ago, I was seriously considering suicide. It's called *ideating*.
Ideating suicide. Have you ever seen a torn-up piñata that some kid just beat

The holy hell out of? Well, that was me. I suppose you're wondering when
I'm going to get back to that word *happiness* again. I'm coming to it.
Listen, the road to happiness is a long fucking road trip. You can't take
The freeway. Back roads, buddy, that's all you got. Unpaved back roads
And bad weather. Storms, baby. Don't expect to get there fast.
        And don't expect yourself or your car to arrive in mint condition.

*

The day I signed my divorce agreement, I found a place built in 1900.
A friend of mine had brought it back to life. There were scars everywhere
On the building. I pictured myself reading a book there, writing one,
Working on a new painting, singing a song, my bare feet stepping on the old,
Forgiving wood floors. *This, this is my new life.*

        Listen to me. Do you think finding a new life is a simple matter?
Finding any life at all is a miracle. There is something inside me that knows
That someday I'll have another dog and I will love, I'll love that dog.
There is something inside me that knows that someday, someone will look
At me and want to touch me—and there will be no hurt in that touch.
There is something inside me that is illogically and profoundly unafraid
Of the word *tomorrow*. There is something inside me that knows
That even though I am getting older by the day, I will always have
The mind of a curious boy who is looking for a whole forest of animals
In the clouds of a summer sky. There is something inside me that has banned
The word *suicide* from the vocabulary of my scarred and battered heart.

                A few nights ago, this guy I know who has become
My friend got a little drunk. It happens. He was in a bad space. (I won't go
        into it.
Everyone deserves some privacy—even a guy who befriends a poet who might
Want to make him the subject of his next poem.) This is the thing: the guy was
In a world where hurt had become the only god that mattered. Tell me
You haven't been there. And tonight, here I am, thinking about my friend.
I have to say that I remain stunned by the beauty of his pain, by his great
And graceful disappointment, by his capacity to feel. *To feel.* Only someone

With deep faith can be that hurt. And I'm sorry I didn't know how to
Tell him that. I think I'll keep that image of him forever. Listen to me.
Everywhere I go, there is all this hurt. I walk away from one world and
      walk
Into another. But everywhere there are faces. The cities of the world
Are teeming with arms and hands that are reaching out to touch.
There is no escaping the pain. There is no escaping the beauty.

God, I've never been this happy. You still want to know what I have to sing
      about?

Meditation on Living in the Desert

NO. 16

Sometimes, at night, desert lizards will crawl on your window as you write.
The light emanating through the glass attracts an array of bugs.
The lizards know this and take full advantage of the situation.

There is a kind of grace to lizards as they flick their tongues and feast.

Living in the desert has taught me to conspire with lizards.

What Remains

At 5:15 in the morning, I walk down to the lobby of a cheap hotel in Albuquerque. Cheap is a description of the hotel—not the price of the room. A seasoned traveler, I expect the van to be late, for the driver to be young, cop an attitude, be inconsiderate. I'm older than I used to be. This can't be helped. Aging is a constant—part of the equation of being alive. Growing up, growing old, dying—this is something that remains.

I ran into someone I hadn't seen in thirty years. She recognized me immediately. I recognized her, too. Something remained of our youth. Something that we recognized in an instant. Maybe it was our smiles. I have never heard a satisfactory explanation for a smile and why we keep doing it. There is something of my last trip that remains loitering in my body. Every time I put on a sport coat, I find something in one of the pockets that tells me where I went the last time I wore it: tickets stubs from a concert, a holy card from a funeral, a receipt from Walgreens, a business card from someone I don't remember meeting.

On my last trip, the young man who drove me to the hotel wasn't interested in helping with my luggage. I'm not an invalid. I don't need a servant. I can carry my own bags. He shot me a look when I didn't fish into my pockets for a five. I'm sure my smile resembled a smirk. You don't have to carry my bags but you don't get a tip for watching. Think again. Rudeness, selfishness, disrespect—name a generation who didn't pass on some of those fine qualities to the next. You have to be mean to survive. You think we only pass on our virtues? Darwin is with me on this one.

*

5:15. At that hour of the morning, I expect to find the lobby empty. Somewhere in the world a monk is praying for the sins of the world. In Burma, they are killing the monks. In 1968, the monks in Vietnam were setting themselves on fire. In the lobby of the cheap hotel, a small-framed man, Latino, nods, my name becomes a question, yes it's me, he takes my bag, calls me sir, the way he says it, a lifetime of *sir* on his lips. I think that maybe he could make a living by giving lessons on the pronunciation of *sir* to young men in their twenties who expect tips for talking on their cell phones. He is awake, happy, talkative: *Ness* he says. What self-respecting Mexican of his generation is named Ness? Nestor? I ask. Yes. Ness is what remains of Nestor. His accent is what remains of his Spanish. *Sir* is what remains of his military training.

To hell with the Rolling Stones, who sang that yesterday didn't matter a damn because it was gone. What the hell is that? Yesterday resides everywhere in our lives. The earth is covered with relics from other centuries: suits of armor from the Crusades, paintings of Madonnas, Egyptian statues, papyri from the time of Christ, vestments of twelfth-century popes. Lucy's bones, Plato's *Republic*, the Torah, the Koran, the Four Gospels, the Popol Vuh. There is a diaspora of Chinese urns dating back to the Ming dynasty scattered in museums all over Europe. Always there are things that remain. What exactly do you think global warming is if not the cumulative remains of our debris in the atmosphere.

Ness asks me where I'm from. When I say El Paso, he smiles, says he lived there in the fifties, asks if the Yselta Bible College is still there. Gone, I say, never heard of it. It remains only in his memory. Fort Bliss, where he was stationed; well, the army and soldiers remain. I think this is supposed to give me comfort. Hell, I'm Catholic, but give me the Yselta Bible College any day.

*

Do you ever wonder what became of Van Gogh's ear? And what, for that matter, happened to the bullet that killed Lincoln? The skin begins to weather like an old worn-out shoe. Perhaps they're better lost, Van Gogh's ear, the bullet. Someone would only sell them on eBay. Worn-out shoes, they're comfortable—but the truth is, they smell. The skin is like that, it begins to crease with use, begins to accumulate decades of odors, and we begin to smell like the lives we have lived. Go ahead, tell that aging woman who put herself through all those face-lifts that yesterday doesn't matter. Her obsession with how she looked yesterday has turned her into a grotesque. Yesterday doesn't matter? Tell that to a smoker dying of lung cancer. Tell that to an alcoholic dying of cirrhosis of the liver. Tell that to any soldier we've sent to fight in one of our wars. Did you think we'd left all those lives behind? Did you really? They're here, trust me, all those ghosts from our past. They skulk around like scorned lovers. Am I scaring you?

And the eyes? They, too, begin to lose the sharp clarity they once had. But there is more to seeing than seeing. I have a theory: the older you get, the better you see. I'll place a bet on that theory. You see, this is a trick. I am not using the word *see* literally. *See* as in *I see* as in *I understand*. Jovita died last week. She outlived a husband and her son, the writer. She was in her nineties. She loved to read, but lost her sight. All she could do was run her hands over the pages of her son's books. Nothing could be done. That's the thing, you begin to lose your body before you die. Hell is letting go of what you were, letting go of all you have ever known yourself to be. In the end, all that remains is your rotting body, and a marble tombstone that says things like

Don't waste any time mourning. Organize.

*

Never mind about my theory. I take back my bet. Maybe we die blind, in the dark, alone, no matter how many friends and relatives are hanging around our deathbed. Jovita, I think she died whispering her son's name. I don't really believe you get wiser as you age. I know a lot of old people who keep electing small-minded, mean-spirited congressmen even as they're flushing down the planet as if it were so much toilet paper. You call that wise? And politics keeps seeping into my poems like poisonous gases from the sewers of New York.

I always wanted to be pure. I always wanted my English to be perfect and iambic. It's too late for someone like me. It's as if I take my words and wash them in the Rio Grande before I place them on my lips or on the page. Washing words in a poor and dirty river is not a good idea. I'm the only human being in the world who thinks my words are clean. I'll never learn. Maybe we never learn anything that matters. Tying your shoes doesn't count. I keep my grandfather's glasses on my desk. I loved my grandfather. That would almost seem like an unnecessary thing to say but I assure you not everyone loves his grandfather—and this because not all grandfathers are worth loving. Of my two grandfathers, one was a sonofabitch if there ever was one. That's the hard truth of it.

I'm lucky. Some people have two grandfathers that are sons of bitches. Look, grandfathers aren't like pears lying in a bin at your local fruit stand. *I'll take that one, the perfect one. Isn't he a beauty?* I've met a lot of hard-core bastards in my day—a good many of them grandfathers. Yeah, I'm lucky. I loved one of my grandfathers. He was wearing his glasses as he lay in his casket and I told my sister Linda, *I want his glasses.* Like a good older sister, she nodded, took charge of the situation: she fearlessly walked up to the casket and gently took off his glasses. It wasn't stealing, not really. What does a dead man need with glasses? I put them on sometimes and squint and say to myself that I am becoming like him, the one grandfather I loved. I've always wondered what he saw when he stared out at his family. It's all just a guessing game no matter how formal the language of our questions. That is what remains: our questions. How and where and who and why, why, why? I see myself a boy, reciting the questions I was taught to memorize: Who made the world? God made the world. Why did God make me? God made me to love, honor, and obey him. The obedience thing got me every time. *We are what we remember.* Someone told me that once. I don't remember who.

Our wars, too, I guess, and how we always manage to turn them into something holy—that's what remains. I want to believe Saint Paul when he says that there are only three things that remain: faith, hope, and love. I've never really approved of Saint Paul's theology, but I want like hell to believe him. And it isn't like I'm alone in wanting to believe that only the beautiful is immortal. I think of Lady Brett, who tells Jake they would have had a damned good time together. I think of Jake's answer: *Isn't it pretty to think so?* I think of Jovita's hands feeling the pages of her son's books. I think of my mother who on the Day of the Dead lays flowers on the graves of the people she's lost. I see the look of sorrow and regret on her face. How many losses can you take before you break? Yeah, I want to believe that in the end only the good will remain. But what are we to make of the woman who had her executor send hate letters to her survivors? What are we to make of Lincoln's bullet? I keep seeing Van Gogh cut off his ear. *Someone would sell it on eBay.* I want to believe that our ability to smile is a sign of our eternal goodness. I want to believe people when they repeat again and again in cities all over the world that love is all that matters.

Isn't it pretty to think so?

Meditation on Living in the Desert

Sometimes I think my tongue is a desert   praying for rain.

A True and Perfect Sound

A voice that is heard is never the same as the
voice that is spoken. As a sound wave travels,
it weakens. It comes across obstacles and is
reflected, refracted, and modified... In the
end, there is no such thing as a true sound or
a true voice.

DANIEL B. SMITH

And there are days when I live on the borders of sanity.
There are days when the voices that speak to me in dreams
Are clearer, louder, more real than the voices that call my name
By day. All my life I've had this dream: I am running
Across a field, running away from someone or *something*
That is intent on killing me. Dreams are made of faceless
Monsters that follow us into dawn. My lungs and legs
Are aching as I run. The ache is all I know. It is forever
Twilight. I exist neither in the day nor in the night.

The green hills of an unknown country stretch out before me—
But the pastoral landscape is just another desert. What good
Is a land of summer to a man who sees and understands and lives
Only in winter? I run. I run. I do not, *cannot* stop. All I can hear
Is the sound, the heaviness, of my own breathing. When I think
I am going to collapse and die, I find refuge in an empty barn.
The barn is quiet, still, serene. It almost seems that I am in a church.
I hear a voice. Is it Gabriel? Is that he? Is the voice inside
Me? Is it mine? And that is when I see my penis lying
On the ground. The penis, the penis that was once attached to
My body is bloody and dirty and the hay and mud are clinging
To it as if it were being transformed into an adobe—something
Made of dirt, something fleshless and inanimate. I want
To pick up my penis and place it back where it belongs. But
Just as I am about to reach down, the door to the barn opens
And the light comes flooding in. I turn my back to the light,

Ashamed. I feel a hand on my back and hear a voice and I know
The voice is speaking but I cannot hear the words. I do not
Know whom the hand belongs to, the hand that's on my shoulder.
I do not know whom the voice belongs to, the voice that is
Giving me words I cannot hear.

                                        Words, sounds, noises,
Monsters. There are voices everywhere. Can you hear them?
Can you hear them? Not only voices in my head and in my dreams
But in the mouths of the people walking down the street. Everyone
Hears voices. What about the voice of the man, younger than I,
Who asks: *Can I help unload your truck? I need some money for a beer.*
What of that voice? What of my voice that answers softly: *I know
What that's like, to need a drink.* What of the voice on the radio
That tells me the name of the song I just listened to? What of
The voice of my mother, who is trying to speak above the quiet
Of her deafness? I'm wondering about hearing aids. I am wondering
What words sound like when they are filtered through a device.
I am listening to the sounds of the day, the sound of the wood floors
Creaking beneath my feet, the sound of a computer tapping out
Words, the sound of an electric drill. The house next door is being
Resurrected. The men say there are ghosts in that old house.
They can hear the voices. Someone left something unsaid.
There are souls who walk this earth with words stuck inside their
Throats. Those words are shrapnel waiting for a surgeon to gently cut
Them out. What if that holy angel never comes? An unspoken
Word—I think I know that sound. There are people I have not
Seen or talked to for years, people whose voices once surrounded
My days with a sound that was almost music. But now those voices
Are gone. I want to call them just to hear the way their words
Transfer wirelessly through the air. Why does that matter? Sound
Is impure, untrue, filtered, indirect. Ask any scientist. He will tell you.
But *now* I want to face the monstrous sound of my own voice.
There are days I live on the borders of sanity. But there are days
The mind is clear like a sky. I woke this morning having had a dream

Of a former life. I am whispering random words into the air.
The random words are transforming themselves into a prayer.
Does my voice sound different now in this new life? Is there
A true sound inside of me? A true and perfect sound? Somewhere?

The Last Meditation on Living in the Desert

I was born in the desert.

I want to die in the desert.

I want to die in the middle of the summer.
At ten o'clock in the morning.
Preferably on the hottest day of the year.
I want everyone who comes to my funeral to keep repeating
Goddamnit it's hot. This will make me smile.
If I am not allowed to smile after I'm dead

then I want to live forever.

But only if I can continue living in the desert.

ABOUT THE AUTHOR

Benjamin Alire Sáenz is a poet, novelist, painter, and writer of children's books. He was born in a small farming community outside of Las Cruces, New Mexico, in 1954, the fourth of seven children. He entered St. Thomas Theological Seminary in Denver, Colorado, in 1972. From 1977 to 1981, he attended the Katholieke Universiteit Leuven in Belgium. He was ordained a Catholic priest for the Diocese of El Paso, Texas, in 1981. In 1984 he left the priesthood and began to pursue a literary career in earnest. Eventually he returned to school and received an M.A. in Creative Writing at the University of Texas at El Paso. He received a fellowship at the University of Iowa to pursue a Ph.D. in American Literature—but his studies at Iowa were interrupted when he received a Wallace Stegner Fellowship in poetry at Stanford University. He spent two years as a Stegner Fellow and was able to complete his first two books, one a collection of poetry, *Calendar of Dust*, and the other a collection of short stories, *Flowers for the Broken*. He continued his Ph.D. studies at Stanford University but returned to the border to teach at UT El Paso before completing his Ph.D. He is currently working on a new book of poems, *Night Disappearing into a Patient Sky*, and is working on a series of paintings entitled *Words on Paper*.

The Chinese character for poetry is made up of two parts: "word" and "temple." It also serves as pressmark for Copper Canyon Press.

Since 1972, Copper Canyon Press has fostered the work of emerging, established, and world-renowned poets for an expanding audience. The Press thrives with the generous patronage of readers, writers, booksellers, librarians, teachers, students, and funders—everyone who shares the belief that poetry is vital to language and living.

Major funding has been provided by:
Amazon.com
Anonymous
Beroz Ferrell & The Point, LLC
Golden Lasso
Lannan Foundation
National Endowment for the Arts
Cynthia Lovelace Sears and Frank Buxton
Washington State Arts Commission

For information and catalogs:
COPPER CANYON PRESS
Post Office Box 271
Port Townsend, Washington 98368
360-385-4925
www.coppercanyonpress.org